Steak, Seafood and Gross Negligence:

Strategic Lessons every CEO Can Learn
from the collapse of the Sizzler restaurant chain

Toby Tatum

Published by eBookIt.com
http://www.eBookIt.com

ISBN-13: 978-1-4566-3811-5

Table of Contents

Foreword 1

Preface 3

Prologue 5

Chapter 1 7
The Early Years

Chapter 2 13
Sizzler Takes Shape

Chapter 3 27
The Decline of Sizzler

Chapter 4 41
Post hoc ergo proctor hoc

Chapter 5 65
Chaos and Collapse

Chapter 6 99
Lessons Learned

Table of Contents

Foreword

I grew up in Los Angles in the nineteen sixties through the nineteen eighties and was a frequent and loyal Sizzler customer. Since then, I have long wondered why Sizzlers just seemed to disappear. Now I know. I loved reading Steak, Seafood and Gross Negligence. It's a great book for two reasons. First, the book provides for the first time since its founding in 1958, a detailed, fascinating insiders behind the scenes story of Sizzler's amazing assent to an incredibly profitable billion-dollar business and then its rapid and shattering decent into bankruptcy. Every CEO should take the time to read this book for the insight to be gained in the formulation of corporate strategy and focus.

Second, every business has the potential for great success or disastrous decline, and too often the only difference is the CEO's ability to develop and execute a winning strategy—which this book is all about. Even though Sizzler started in 1958, the Sizzler story presented here bear lessons in the practice of management that are highly relevant today for all CEOs. These Sizzler lessons in strategy and focus apply to every industry, but this book is simply a MUST-READ for those in the restaurant industry.

–David Fein, MBA, CEO ValuSource

Preface
August 1998

For a moment in time, the world stands still when it learns about the crash of a commercial airliner. No doubt the thought racing through people's minds is "there but for the grace of God go I." In the aftermath of these events there is always an investigation to find out what went wrong. The ultimate purpose of such investigations being, of course, to further improve the design of aircraft or flight procedures so as to ensure another aircraft will not go down for the same reason.

The cumulative effect of this disaster postmortem, repeated subsequent to every crash throughout most of the world has contributed greatly to an improvement in the safety of air travel. However, when a major corporation employing thousands of people shuts it doors there is no organized, systematic attempt by any central authority to find out what went wrong. Indeed, excluding some modest attempts by trade publications to initiate a cursory examination as to why a particular company crashed and burned, there is seldom a permanent published record of the disaster's cause. This is unfortunate. I believe much can be learned from such an exercise and that is the purpose of this book

Throughout my career as a business owner and manager, I made an effort to read most of the popular books on the practice of management that came on the market. I read many of Tom Peters works starting with *In Search of Excellence*, Michael Porter's *Competitive Strategy* and *Competitive Advantage*, Lee Iococa's autobiographical account of how he saved the Chrysler Corporation plus dozens of others. In addition, I read a substantial number of some relatively more esoteric books pertaining to such subjects as Total Quality Management, Statistical Quality Control, Strategic Planning, Consumer Research and so on. I also attended numerous seminars on topics such as Leadership, Personnel Management, Labor Law and a host of others. All of these books and seminars pretty much belonged to the "how to" genre of literature and I found them enormously beneficial. I applied what I learned as best I could over the years and I believe forged a solid, well-run company in the process.

However, despite my efforts to stay abreast of the latest thinking in the practice of management and apply what I learned throughout my twenty-two-year career as the President of my own company, in the end I had to hastily liquidate my company's assets in a desperate effort to avoid bankruptcy. As a franchised operator of Sizzler restaurants, I was joined at the hip so to speak with the franchisor, Sizzler Restaurants International. As that organization began to sink, I was ultimately pulled down with it.

Although the Sizzler restaurant chain still exists, it is not much more than a mere shadow of its former self. Over the last few years since I liquidated my company, many people have asked me why Sizzler came apart. This book is my response to those inquiries. It is an account of my experience as the franchised owner/operator of Sizzler restaurants and my view of how this once very successful restaurant chain came undone. One could describe this book, I suppose, as a how-not-to book. As such, I believe it can be very worthwhile reading for any practicing manager or Chief Executive. It is an investigation into an avoidable manmade disaster. I believe by understanding the mistakes made by Sizzler's senior management, one can become better equipped to avoid the same mistakes or become more sensitive to the implications of similar weaknesses in one's own organization and what they portend if not addressed and corrected.

Prologue

On Sunday[1], June 2nd, 1996 Sizzler Restaurants International filed for Chapter 11 bankruptcy protection and closed one hundred thirty of its two hundred fifteen corporate owned stores. As a result of this action, approximately four thousand six hundred people lost their jobs. The notice these individuals received of their termination came from security guards Sizzler arranged to bar their entry to the closed restaurants as they arrived for work throughout the day on Monday, June 3rd.

Just four years earlier, sales from combined corporate and franchised operations exceeded 1.1 billion Dollars. Sizzler International owned and operated approximately two hundred twenty restaurants in the United States and an additional thirty-five stores in Australia and New Zealand. In addition, there were four hundred forty-one Sizzlers owned and operated by franchisees throughout the U.S., plus units in Puerto Rico, Thailand, Taiwan, Japan, Australia, Kuwait and Saudi Arabia. Although Sizzler's expansion did not parallel the growth of such giants as McDonalds, Burger King, Taco Bell or Kentucky Fried Chicken, it was nevertheless one of the true industry leaders for its market segment and highly regarded by securities analyst.

How could such a successful and expanding restaurant chain like Sizzler crumble so quickly? This disastrous collapse of a once successful chain is reminiscent of similar events such as Sambos and Victoria Station.

By accounts published in various restaurant industry trade journals, one can surmise that the beginning of the end for Sizzler coincided with the introduction of its *Buffet Court* repositioning strategy. However, from my prospective as a second-generation Sizzler Franchisee with over thirty years involvement with the organization I can say that the introduction of the Buffet Court was not the cause of Sizzler's decline *per se* but one symptom of the cause.

As a multi-unit Sizzler franchisee and fifteen-year member of the Board of Trustees of the National Sizzler Franchisee Association, I had the opportunity to view the rise and fall of Sizzler from a front row seat. I developed a close working relationship with most of the multi-unit Sizzler franchisees across the country as well as Sizzler International Senior Management. My professional career for twenty-two years was that of an owner/ operator of Sizzler Restaurants and I had no plans to do anything other than operate Sizzlers until such time that I should chose to retire. All of that changed in the winter of nineteen ninety-four when I reset my course and began to liquidate my restaurants either by selling them as going concerns or closing them down. By late nineteen ninety-five I

---

[1] Yes, Sunday. Unusual for the court to be open for business on a Sunday, but not impossible.

was completely out of the Sizzler Business and watched from the sidelines as nearly all the other Sizzler franchisees whom I came to know over the years either closed their stores voluntarily and liquidated their operating equipment and leaseholds or filed for bankruptcy.

Chapter 1
The Early Years

On January 27th, 1958 Del and Helen Johnson opened a small restaurant in Airport Village, a sort of "farmers market" shopping arcade in Culver City, California, near Los Angeles International Airport. They called their restaurant *Del's Sizzler Steak House*. Their restaurant was nestled in among several other restaurants offering a variety of products including tacos, pizza, hamburgers, chicken and fish & chips.

Del's and Helen's idea was to sell steak and potato dinners using a "fast food" merchandising approach. The idea being that people would stand in line, order off a wall-hung menu board placed behind the service counter offering a *very* limited menu featuring four items: a top sirloin steak, New York steak, hamburger steak and steak sandwich with choice of French fries or baked potato. "We offered a 'first class salad," according to Del [2] but we served Commercial Grade meat--we had to in order to sell a steak for 99 cents." When the customer's order was prepared, the cook would call out that customer's order number and the customer would then go to the cook's "pick-up window" retrieve his meal and return to his table.

In addition to the operational format, the Johnsons believed that the name by which the restaurant would be known was also a key ingredient to success. "Helen and I were trying to think of a name; a single syllable name," remembers Del.[3] "Something that would merchandise well. In the old days, they served steaks on those sizzling platters. In a first-class restaurant, when you ordered steak, they'd bring it out, put the butter on that steak and that plate was hot, it was aluminum and it would sizzle when they put it down in front of you. That's how we came up with the name. I knew we wanted to use those sizzling platters."

With this idea in mind, Del and Helen proceeded to set up their restaurant. Circumstances at that time found them with very little money. "All we had was fifty dollars some friends loaned to us." Helen told me. "We set our restaurant up as cheaply as possible. For dining room tables, we used old picnic benches and tables. I covered them with red oil cloth and made red and white curtains for the windows. The building we were in was originally an auto repair garage and the floor was black top pavement. We couldn't afford new flooring or carpeting so we did the cheapest thing we could think of; we covered the dining room floor with sawdust." A friendly competitor in the village by the name of Jim Collins who

---

[2] Unpublished hand out provided attendees to Sizzler's 25 Year Anniversary Celebration

[3] ibid.

owned an operation called Hamburger Handout, helped Del and Helen get started by buying them some restaurant equipment and light fixtures.

With this austere beginning, another mom-n-pop restaurant was open for business in Los Angeles. What was remarkable about this little restaurant was that it was the only one of its kind in existence--it was the world's first budget family steak house. And the concept was well received. Having survived their first year--which is never a given in the restaurant business--Del decided to run a one-cent anniversary sale: Buy one steak at the regular price and get the second one for a penny. "We opened at 11:00 a.m. and stayed open until 9:00 p.m. People were lined up all the way around the building," says Helen. On the first day of the sale, the Johnsons sold 1,050 steak dinners; on the second day they sold 1,200.

By nineteen sixty the Johnsons had opened two more Sizzlers; one in Redondo Beach, California and one in Gardena. "Then my buddy, Jay W. Thomason--who I had worked for years ago," Del explained, "over in Highland Park--had a coffee shop that wasn't doing very well and I said 'Jay, let's convert it to a Sizzler-type operation.' So, we converted Jay's store. Then he opened a second Sizzler. One day about a year later--this was after we'd been in operation about two years--I said to Jay, 'Let's go to the bank, put down a thousand dollars apiece and start a new corporation for franchising.' I took him in as an equal partner and we went to Crocker Bank and opened up a new account. We went from there to an attorney to set up the franchising corporation."[4]

With that, the Johnsons along with Jay Thomason began selling Sizzler franchises. For an office, the Johnsons enclosed the breezeway between their house and garage. They had one employee at the office who was Bob Minshew, Sr., Del's nephew. Bob was their controller. Bob Sr. would eventually leave the employ of his uncle and open a Sizzler restaurant of his own. From this beginning, he acquired a multi-state franchise development agreement and opened several Sizzlers. After his retirement, his son Bob Minshew Jr. took over the helm of this company and built it up to become the largest franchise operation in the company with approximately forty-two Sizzlers in four states.

With their breezeway converted to Sizzler Franchise Sales headquarters, Del and Helen met with prospective franchisees including my father and mother, Cecil and Harriet Tatum. In addition to using this makeshift office to sell Sizzler franchises, they also used it as a training center. This is where my parents were taught how to keep daily sales and cost records on a manual worksheet the Johnsons designed. In addition to that, in some cases during this one-week training period, the new Sizzler franchisees would stay as guests in the Johnson's home. My mother recalls that she and my dad stayed there for several days. "The Johnsons were wonderful people," my mother recalls, "and, they had a dog named 'Sizzler'."

---

[4] ibid.

In nineteen sixty-three my parents purchased Sizzler Franchise number 46. It was a six-page document printed in twelve-point type that said little more than they had the right to operate a Sizzler in Santa Rosa, California, and had to abide by the Sizzler format. Oh, and one more thing; they had to make Heinz Catsup available for customers. These were truly the early days of franchising. It would not be until nineteen seventy-nine that the Federal Trade Commission would enact laws regulating franchising and requiring appropriate disclosures to would-be franchisees. For anyone who has had the opportunity to read a current Franchisor's Franchise Offering Circular or Franchise License Agreement set in six-point type on legal paper, they would be amazed at the relative informality of a vintage Sizzler franchise agreement.

Upon obtaining a Sizzler franchise, and completing one week of on-site training at the Sizzler in Wilmington Beach, California my parents moved from Los Angeles to Santa Rosa, in the heart of the Northern California Wine Country.[5] They located a vacant lot across the street from a new shopping center under construction and negotiated a build-to-suit lease with Hugh Codding, the property owner, for a Sizzler Prototype structure of approximately thirty-five hundred square feet. Six months later they were open for business. The date of the Grand Opening was November 21st, 1963--the day before President Kennedy was assassinated.

On that same day an ad appeared in The Press Democrat, Santa Rosa's only daily paper. It advertised a Top Sirloin Steak Dinner including choice of French fries or baked potato for $1.29 ($.99 on Monday Night); New York Steak Dinner, $1.39; Ground Beef Platter, $.69; Steak Sandwich $.69; 1/4 lb. Hamburger Sandwich $.39; and Tossed Green Salad, $.19. All children's meals sold at 1/2 price.

On hand to provide training in Sizzler operation and assist with the challenges of a restaurant Grand Opening were Del and Helen Johnson. They stayed in Santa Rosa for a week helping my parents get started. To everyone's satisfaction and pleasure, the Grand Opening was successful and the daily sales level immediately established itself above break even. The customers came for the budget steaks but seemed to be equally fascinated with the sawdust covered floors and wall decorations consisting of mounted Bull Horns and one huge oil painting of a bull hanging prominently on one wall in the dining room. With that, a family business was launched which would be passed from parents to sons and continue for the next thirty-two years

The Johnsons continued to operate the four Sizzlers they owned and sell Sizzler franchises throughout the nineteen sixties. Restaurant concept franchising began to burgeon during this decade and as Sizzler's began to pop up mainly in California but here

---

[5] During this one-week training period, I joined my parents for a day. At the age of 17, this was my first exposure to the restaurant business. I received a day's training in how to wash dishes and carry out the garbage.

and there throughout the country, other restaurant franchises were also starting to spring up around the country.

Another individual who was actively engaged in selling restaurant franchises during the late fifties and early sixties was a man who called himself Colonel Sanders. In these early days of franchising, Colonel Sanders was not trying to put people into fast food restaurants per se. His idea, one he sold personally by going door to door to various restaurants, was to persuade these pre-existing restaurant owners on the proposition of selling his product in their stores in addition to whatever else they were then selling. What the Colonel had to offer was his own special recipe for fried chicken. If a restaurateur went for his proposition, a chicken fryer would be retrofitted into the client's restaurant, and up would go Colonel Sanders Kentucky Fried Chicken merchandising paraphernalia along with take-out containers for the product also emblazoned with the Colonel's logo. The store operator would then prepare fried chicken using the Colonel's secret combination of spices and serve it in the Colonel's trade-marked containers all of which they had to buy from the Colonel.

One of the first restaurants to subscribed to Colonel Sanders program in Southern California was a place called Dinah's, also located in Airport Village near the Johnson's Sizzler. In what one may now perhaps consider one of the world's biggest little mistakes in judgment, Dinah tired of the Colonel's program and decided to end her short-lived franchise arrangement with him. However, the owner of the hamburger stands next door to Dinah's thought differently of the Colonel's program. This was Jim Collins, the man who helped the Johnsons go into business. When Jim learned that Dinah was terminating her Kentucky Fried Chicken franchise, he got in touch with the Colonel and arranged to take over where Dinah left off. So, into Dinah's he went, disconnected the chicken fryer, stacked up all the Kentucky Fried Chicken paper carry-out containers and whatever chicken Dinah still had on hand and moved everything next door to his place--and presto--Jim Collins was a franchisee of Colonel Sanders' Kentucky Fried Chicken.

At the time Jim was in the process of moving the Kentucky Fried Chicken merchandise out of Dinah's and into his Hamburger Handout, he had bigger ideas. This was not his only hamburger stand. By this time, he had three Hamburger Handouts in the Los Angeles area and aspirations to have more. In fact, his original idea was to emulate another fast-food place he had visited. As fate would have it, Jim, who had recently graduated from UCLA with a degree in Engineering, was working as the on-site structural engineer for a church being built in San Bernardino. This church was being built near a hamburger stand that was doing an impressive business and Jim thought of trying to imitate this hamburger stand operation elsewhere in Southern California. The operation he tried to copy was owned and operated by two brothers who simply gave the name of their hamburger stand their own last name. They called their little place "McDonalds."

Soon after Jim Collins began selling Colonel Sanders Kentucky Fried Chicken out of his Hamburger Handout operation in Airport Village, he replicated the arrangement in his other two hamburger stands. Before long, his Kentucky Fried Chicken was outselling his hamburgers and he started selling the chicken exclusively. In fact, the Kentucky Fried Chicken was selling so well, Jim started opening up more outlets dedicated exclusively to selling that product. Each new outlet Jim opened did well and realizing he had a good thing going, Jim kept on opening additional Kentucky Fried Chicken outlets throughout the greater Los Angeles area. This process continued unabated and within ten years, Jim Collins was the largest owner of Kentucky Fried Chicken franchise restaurants in the world. Eventually, Jim would come to own, altogether, somewhere close to two hundred Kentucky Fried Chicken operations in California, Florida, Oregon, Texas, and Illinois plus 90 units in Queensland, Australia.

In nineteen sixty-seven, Del and Helen Johnson felt it was time to retire so Del approached Jim Collins and asked if he would be interested in purchasing the Sizzler Family Steak House chain. Jim accepted the offer and teamed up with Walt McBee, who was then the Executive Vice President of Jim's business. Together, Jim and Walt called on their mutual friend and former UCLA fraternity brother Rush Backer and invited him to be a third participant in the acquisition of the Sizzler chain. Rush came on board and together, the three partners bought the Sizzler chain which at that time consisted of four restaurants wholly owned by the Johnsons and one hundred sixty franchised Sizzlers.

By the time the Johnsons retired, the restaurant concept they invented was spreading rapidly throughout the country. From their modest beginning a new genre of restaurants altogether known as "budget family steak houses" had emerged. Eventually this market segment would become populated with numerous "copycat" concepts. Many of Sizzler's competitors have come and gone, but more than a few have survived and prospered. To the best of my recollection, the first to copy Sizzler was a concept called Toppers. Soon to follow were Happy Steak, Mr. Steak, Western Sizzlin', Ponderosa, Bonanza, Golden Corral, Ryan's, Rustler, Western Steer, Quincy's and others--but *Del's Sizzler Steak House* was the first.

Chapter 2
Sizzler Takes Shape

Rush Backer, also an engineer, was installed as Sizzler's President, and therewith the company launched an aggressive expansion program both in franchised operations and company owned units expanding across the U.S. outwardly from Southern California. By this time, Jim had vertically integrated his company by starting up a wholly owned subsidiary, Collins Food Service, which was a wholesale food distribution company servicing all of this KFC's and Sizzlers. The parent company, known as Collins Foods International went public in November, 1968. Shortly after this event, Jim hired Richard P. Birmingham, the C.P.A. from Arthur Andersen who helped Jim acquire Sizzler from the Johnsons, and put him in charge of the wholesale food distribution branch of the company.

Throughout the nineteen-sixties and most of the nineteen-seventies, the basic Sizzler concept changed very little. About the only significant change was discontinuing to spread sawdust on the dining room floor in the mid nineteen-sixties and the introduction of "Sizzler Dining Room Service" in the early nineteen-seventies.

In nineteen seventy-two, right after I graduated from San Francisco State University with a Master's Degree in Business Administration, my parents decided to retire from the restaurant business and offered to sell the one Sizzler they owned to me and my brother. Neither of us had any money so we agreed to pay our mom and dad $1,333.33 a month for ten years. When my brother Tom and I bought out our parents, we had eleven employees and owned a restaurant doing approximately $300,000 a year in sales. We would eventually build our company to one consisting of six Sizzlers, employing two hundred seventy-five employees and serving approximately a million customers a year.

During the nineteen-seventies, Sizzler was a budget family steak house--period. The featured steaks were the top sirloin and New York cut. The menu was very limited and the operation was reasonably simple to run. Sizzler purchased portion controlled below-USDA Choice grade meat and emphasized low price over high quality. Food costs during these early years hovered in the mid forty percent range and direct labor ran around twelve to fifteen percent while retail prices remained well below those of full-service restaurants featuring comparable products.

One event I believe probably worked to Sizzler's advantage was the recession that plagued the nation in the mid nineteen-seventies--roughly nineteen seventy-four through nineteen seventy-five. This recession was the most severe since the depression of the nineteen thirties. Consumers suffered very sharp declines in disposable income during this period and, as is typical under such circumstances, made necessary adjustments in their buying patterns and life style. I think, Sizzler--at least in California where the predominate number of its units were located--benefited in the long run from this realignment of spending patterns as people, still wanting to go out for a steak dinner, now had an alternative to the full service, higher priced white table cloth restaurants. This not to say that Sizzler's market share burgeoned during this recession. In fact, these were difficult times and it was a struggle to get through them. However, after the recession had worked its way through the economy and incomes started once again to rise, many people by this time found the convenience and lower prices of budget steak restaurants sufficiently to their liking that they remained loyal customers thereafter.

In part, this broadening of Sizzler's customer base can be attributed to Sizzler's move toward higher quality meat, and its departure from self-service to Sizzler's version of dining room wait staff service as the nineteen-seventies drew to a close. Some new menu items were added including the introduction of Prime Rib and Sizzler's novel introduction of "combination platters" such as Steak & Malibu Chicken, Steak & Shrimp and Steak & Langostino[6] to compliment the original combination platter featuring Steak & Lobster we introduced earlier in the decade with a retail price of $2.99.

Sizzler was probably the first restaurant chain to make Prime Rib and Steak & Lobster available at budget prices. To do this, wholesale buyers working for Sizzler shopped the entire world for lobster tails. We were getting lobster from Brazil, Australia, Russia, Venezuela, and other countries I can't recall. In the process, we became experts on the peculiarities of lobster harvested from different regions--especially the differences between cold water lobster and warm water lobster. Moreover, we had to learn the hard way about proper and improper harvesting techniques--the latter yielding a tail from a shocked animal that resulted in a cooked product which emitted a very noticeable ammonia smell. It took us years to figure out the reason for the customer complaints we got from time to time regarding spoiled lobster tails when we knew there had been no mishandling on our part as store operators.

Along with this evolutionary upgrading in product quality--primarily red meat, the addition of new menu items, and therewith operating cost structure, there was a movement toward upgrading and remodeling the physical facilities which really exploded in the early nineteen-eighties. This was Sizzler's first formal effort at repositioning the concept. It worked quite well and seemed to ingrain the organization with the notion that repositioning is necessary from time to time and, moreover, something senior management knew how to do. However, the single biggest change to overcome Sizzler in the late nineteen-seventies and nineteen-eighties was in advertising.

---

[6] Langostino is a Spanish word with different meanings in different areas. In the United States, it is commonly used in the restaurant trade to refer to the meat of the squat lobster, which is neither a true lobster nor a prawn. Squat lobsters are more closely related to porcelain and hermit crabs.

In the early nineteen-seventies Sizzler's growth in California made possible the pooling of advertising dollars generated from each operating unit--both corporate owned and franchised. It quickly became evident that one of the single greatest advantages of being part of a franchised operation was the enormous economy of scale in advertising expenditures available to each operating unit. Anybody could copy the Sizzler merchandising format exactly and advertise under some other name. However, fifteen thousand dollars, for example, a year expended in advertising by an independent operation buys exactly fifteen thousand dollars' worth of advertising. The same per unit expenditure in a franchised operation in theory and largely in realty buys *each and every unit* in a geographical market, advertising worth fifteen thousand dollars a year *times* the number of stores in the market--*especially* once an amount of money required to breach the television threshold is achieved. Put another way, once an ability to maintain a continuous advertising presence on television is breached, that is to say, the ability to air approximately a dozen thirty second commercials on television every week of the year, *each* individual restaurant within reach of the TV station's signal in, for example the San Francisco Bay Area, will experience an advertising presence in excess of *two hundred thousand dollars a month*! Thus, *each* operating unit comes to enjoy a quantity and quality of advertising within its small geographical territory whose cost substantially exceeds its entire gross sales.

Very quickly, everyone in Sizzler--both corporate management and franchisees alike-- became intensely aware of the power of television advertising. Initially, Sizzler employed the advertising agency of Hall, Butler and Blatherwick who serviced the Sizzler account from nineteen seventy-one to nineteen seventy-six. By this time, only Dick Butler remained active in this relatively small ad agency and he sold out to BBDO, one of the giants in the industry.

About four years prior to Sizzler being adopted by BBDO, the corporation hired Michael M. Minchin as its Vice President of Marketing. By virtue of Mr. Minchin's extensive marketing, advertising and executive skills and experience coupled with the central role that TV advertising was beginning to play in Sizzler, he quickly rose in prominence as the number two man in Sizzler, as the company's Executive Vice President.

Sizzler was originally structured as a subsidiary of Collins Foods International, a publicly traded corporation wherein resided all of Jim Collin's Kentucky Fried Chicken franchises. As such the President of Sizzler reported to the President of CFI. Up until 1974, this post was occupied by Jim Collins however at that time he brought in a senior KFC executive by the name of Norm Haberman to take over that position. Jim Collins, then held the solitary title of Chairman of the Board. Mr. Haberman served as CEO of Collins Foods International from August 1974 to December, 1979 then left to become President of Denny's; a position he subsequently left within months of making that career move. Upon Mr. Haberman's departure, Jim Collins reassumed the role of Chief Executive Officer but it appeared he more or less assigned hands-on oversight of CFI to

Richard P. Birmingham, whose official title was Chief Executive Officer of Collins Food Service, the company's wholesale food distribution division. Throughout this era, another key senior manager was Dave Gaon, Sizzler's primary in-house legal counsel. During this time period it was Mr. Gaon who was the principal corporate contact with Sizzler franchisees. The franchisees' relationship with Mr. Gaon was not always cordial and there was a growing undercurrent of dissatisfaction with him among the franchisees which would eventually be resolved in a way that would have a significant impact within the franchise community.

Another organization to spring up in the nineteen-seventies was the National Sizzler Franchisee Association. The National Sizzler Franchisee Association was formed by Vincent Liuzza, the Sizzler franchisee in New Orleans, in response to his concern about some early warning signs of potential Franchisor abuse of power. As Vincent tells it, "We were ready to begin construction on our second Sizzler in New Orleans and I was advised that I had to use the one and only general contractor approved by the franchisor. I realized at that moment that I and all franchisees needed some sort of protection." With that, Vince contacted as many multi-unit Sizzler owners as he could and a meeting was convened at the Royal Sonesta Hotel on Bourbon Street in the French Quarter in June 1973. From that austere beginning, a franchisee organization was forged whose influence within Sizzler, both among all franchisees and senior Sizzler management, would eventually grow to become substantial.[7]

However, in the beginning, Vince Liuzza's initiative was not met with open arms by the franchisor. Indeed, the franchisor made an effort to quell the initiative by forming a Franchisee Advisory Committee, funded by the franchisor and staffed with franchisees selected by them. Vince said he would support Sizzler's efforts to form a Franchisee Advisory Committee but he would not agree to their request that he therewith abandon support of the National Sizzler Franchisee Association.

Sizzler's Franchisee Advisory Committee was formed nevertheless and held two or three meetings. That committee never took hold and no additional meetings ever took place. On the other hand, the NSFA held a second meeting in Las Vegas about a year later—nineteen seventy-four. In the interim there was an attempt to form yet another franchisee association among some of the disgruntled franchisees who wanted to sue Sizzler for some of their perceived abuse at the hands of the franchisor. Although this group hired an attorney to assist them in their effort, they were not well organized and the project failed.

The mission of the NSFA on the other hand, which was crystallized in Las Vegas, was fundamentally to promote and enhance communication between senior Sizzler

---

[7] I was elected by the franchisee membership to serve as a Trustee of the NSFA in 1979, a position I held until I left the Sizzler organization in 1994. It was through my position as a Trustee of the NSFA that I got to know many Sizzler franchisees around the country and came to know all of Sizzler's senior management pretty much on a first name basis.

management and the franchise community. Vince made every effort to keep it from becoming a platform from which to launch anti-franchisor initiatives and this fact is no doubt why the organization eventually came to serve such an important role in the growth and success of the chain.

Without regard for the underlying purpose in forming the NSFA or its mission, the relationship between the franchise community and Sizzler's principal contact, Dave Gaon, continued to be somewhat rancorous. The problem was resolved in the franchisees favor when Mr. Gaon was dismissed by Dick Birmingham sometime early in nineteen eighty. This made Dick Birmingham a hero in the eyes of the franchisees and significantly improved both the quality of the system's franchisor/franchisee relationship and the credibility of the National Sizzler Franchisee Association. One of the long-term outcomes of this single event, I believe was a diminished ability or unwillingness among many franchisees to be adequately objective about some of Dick Birmingham's short comings which I will discuss later

Rush Backer retired as Sizzler's President in nineteen eighty and was replaced by Tom Gregory. Tom Gregory's was hired in nineteen seventy-four to serve as Sizzler's Vice President of Operations, a position he held for about four or five years before being moved to the North East on special assignment to develop that market for Sizzler. Tom brought to the position of President much successful experience in the hospitality industry including having served as the executive assistant to Woodrow Marriott, Senior Vice President of the Marriott Corporation and having been employed as Vice President of A & W Food Service of Canada.

Tom Gregory's return to Los Angeles as President of Sizzler in nineteen eighty can pretty much be described as the beginning of Sizzler's Golden Decade. Tom was the *only* person in Sizzler's history up to that time to serve in a senior management position who had a senior management hospitality industry background or any prior experience working with franchisees.

Tom Gregory was an effective executive and I don't want to minimize the influence he had on Sizzler's tremendous growth through the nineteen-eighties. However, Tom took over the reins of Sizzler at time when a substantial number of factors had become aligned such that the restaurant chain was uniquely well positioned for success.

By this time, the semi-self-service budget family steak house concept had become widely accepted by the dining out public. To be sure, Sizzler had many competitors by this time but largely outside of California, the venue where the majority of Sizzler's units were located. Sizzler owned the budget steak house niche throughout Southern California from Ventura County to San Diego and the greater San Francisco Bay Area. This market ownership included a commanding advertising budget which enabled the chain to break through the television advertising threshold in the two most populated regions of the state. This capability has so far proven to be impossible for any other direct competitors.

The cash flow from Sizzler's company owned units, primarily in California, coupled with the franchise fees being collected was enormous--eventually approaching one million dollars a week--and it provided the funds to further develop the concept outside California without any debt financing. Realizing that *the* key competitive advantage for restaurants in this market niche was the capability to have a continuous presence on television, Sizzler's strategy for the development of corporate owned stores was to rapidly develop ADIs (Area of Dominant Influence) i.e., geographical markets defined by the reach of the three television network affiliates--ABC, NBC and CBS where, additionally, around four percent of gross sales budgeted for advertising from the number of units Sizzler could reasonably expect to open in the market could accomplish that objective. With that, Sizzler went after the Phoenix market and the Baltimore / Washington D.C. market. The latter market was attacked with one fell swoop as Sizzler acquired approximately eighty Rustler Steak House restaurants and converted most of them into Sizzlers.

Not all the markets Sizzler attempted to develop met with success. Several Sizzlers were opened then closed in Kansas City and Houston. The company also made an attempt to work its magic in the Atlanta market but ran up against very strong competition and was never able to make it more than an also-ran.

Sizzler also experienced an enormous stroke of good luck in the mid-nineteen-seventies by way of the support it received from its advertising agency. Ray Coen, Hall, Butler and Blatherwicks' Vice President and Senior Account Executive was placed in charge of the Sizzler Account. Working closely with Mike Minchin, together Mike and Ray forged a product development, advertising and promotion program for the chain that the competition just could not touch. To this capability, Ray Coen played a leadership role in implementing one additional and very significant competitive advantage on Sizzler's behalf.

When it comes to television advertising, the things most evident to the casual observer are the product, the story board by which the product message is delivered and of course, product price. However, under Ray Coen's direction, Sizzler was able to enjoy a more subtle benefit from its television advertising--something with which no other competitor in the country could compete at that time. This was the subliminal effect on the television viewer within the advertising message delivered by way of the food photography.

Hall, Butler and Blatherwick became the advertising industry pioneer and expert in the development of close-up, true color, fast action and slow-motion food photography and it accomplished all of this on behalf of Sizzler. Today, this sort of photography in television commercials is common place. But in the mid nineteen-seventies, Sizzler was the only

18

restaurant chain advertising on TV with this capability. Eventually, of course, the advertising industry would learn to copy this agency's achievement but for several years, Sizzler had this advantage all to itself.

In nineteen seventy-six, BBDO, a giant in the advertising agency business, bought Hall, Butler and Blatherwick. However, Ray Coen came with the deal and remained on for several more years as Sizzler's Senior Agency Account Executive. Thus, as far a Sizzler was concerned, this was more or less, a non-event.

With the advent of the nineteen-eighties, the Sizzler chain's senior management, mid-level store operations management and most of its franchised owner/operators were seasoned veterans. Operational skills among this group were, for the most part, well developed. Moreover, a very large number of the franchised operations across the country were owned and operated by multi-unit franchisees and this group was comprised of some very experienced, sophisticated and well-educated individuals. The contribution to Sizzler's success made by this group was immense, primarily through our ability to effectively manage our units and grow our respective geographical markets with little or no need for direction or support from the franchisor. And as the franchisees grew their respective geographical markets each new unit that opened added an additional thirty to fifty thousand dollars a year into Sizzler's advertising pool.

And, we were team players. After all, why mess with success? So long as the Sizzler formula was working, the multi-unit franchise operators became one of Sizzler's most powerful allies by which to maintain uniformity in concept execution and cooperation in making necessary changes to the concept from time to time.

In addition, for the most part, the debt service incumbent on the franchised operators throughout the system was relatively low. Sizzler International, in fact, had *no* debt service obligation. Thus, when it became apparent that most of the stores in the chain, many of them built in the nineteen-sixties needed a face lift, the entire system, corporate stores and franchised alike, were ready, willing and able to make the required changes. System wide, millions upon millions of dollars were spent remodeling, enlarging and re-equipping the existing stores throughout the country in this concept repositioning adventure. We were already flush with cash and the consumer reaction to our remodeling efforts was a resounding success. Once a store was remodeled, an increase in sales was an absolute certainty.

The creative flair with which Sizzler corporate and franchisees pursued the remodeling of their units in the early and mid-nineteen-eighties was something to behold. In retrospect I can say that a good portion of the money spent on these projects often exceeded what was reasonably appropriate. We all became somewhat disconnected from reality as we tried to outdo one another in the lavishness we bestowed on our budget steak houses. To a large degree, the projects became monuments to our egos and if someone somewhere managed to retrofit more brass and glass in their store than we had in ours, it became a point of honor to outdo them on our next remodeling. And, if this were not enough, when it came time to build a new store from the ground up, the cost of doing so climbed quickly into the stratosphere. Without regard to the cost to remodel or build new units, the mind set throughout the system was so what? Our expected return on investment from these undertakings was so high we could afford to trade a little future cash for respectability among our peers.

At the same time that this massive remodeling effort was initiated throughout the system, there was another change taking place as well. This was the introduction of the "Sizzler Salad Bar." I put that in quotes because by this time, most Sizzlers already had salad bars. However, they were modest things, approximately eight feet long by four feet wide, constructed of plywood with a wood veneer used for exterior home siding. The containers holding the lettuce and vegetables were kept chilled by being inset into a bed of crushed ice that was replaced daily. This innovation had worked its way into Sizzler by the late nineteen-seventies and it was well received but didn't do anything to appreciably change the consumers' impression of Sizzler as a budget family steak house.

However, the introduction of the Sizzler Salad Bar changed things a lot. These salad bars were monsters. They ranged anywhere from twelve to fourteen feet long and six feet wide, with lavish applications of tile, decorative lighting, brass and glass and self-contained refrigeration systems. The cost of these free-standing salad bars started at around twenty-five thousand dollars and depending on the size and materials used in construction could easily climb well above that figure. But here again, the attitude was so what? By installing these salad bars, we were effectively repositioning Sizzler from simply a budget family steak house to Sizzler Steak, Seafood and Salad Bar. The Sizzler Salad Bar enabled us to capture a new market segment, the healthy eater and at the same time hold onto our budged steak niche. Sales increases persisted unabated, year after year throughout the nineteen-eighties. A store with an annual sales increase over the preceding year of less than ten percent was considered an underachiever. The Sizzler Restaurant Chain and most of the franchisees in it considered themselves, within their respective markets, as king of the hill.

Although Sizzler franchisees were all big fish within our various regional markets, there was one franchisee among us who was the undisputed King of the Sizzler Franchisees. His name was Jack Williams. Jack was originally a senior operations manager for the franchisor but left that position to become the managing partner for an investment group comprised of three other individuals. Together this group owned a company called FORBCO and their mission was to develop a geographic territory they had sequestered for themselves within the heart of the Greater Los Angeles region, Sizzler's strongest market. And, under Jack's direction, develop it they did. At one time I believe FORBCO was the franchised owner/operator of thirty-five Sizzlers and was enjoying annual sales of around of sixty million dollars.

Jack Williams could best be described as the entrepreneur's entrepreneur. He had a sort of feel for what was right for Sizzler that could not be matched by anyone else in the system, either within senior corporate management, other franchisees or BBDO's marketing experts. Plus, on the operational side of things, he ran a tight ship. All of his stores were well managed and capable of executing the Sizzler concept very effectively. Jack was a master restaurateur, a very charismatic individual, President of the National Sizzler Franchisee Association, and confidant of senior Sizzler management. He made FORBCO a shining example of how to run Sizzlers which almost all Sizzler franchisees and corporate management respected and aspired to imitate. In fact, it would be hard to overstate the positive influence Jack Williams imparted to the Sizzler Restaurant Chain. He created a vision of what the chain could become and imbued in the franchisees a degree of confidence in what we were about and what more we could achieve that was truly one of the central driving forces in Sizzler's rapid expansion through the nineteen-eighties. As O'Neill Printy, a ten-unit franchisee in the Silicon Valley put it, "Jack Williams was the sole of Sizzler."

Moreover, there is no question but that Jack was the creator and outspoken advocate for the development and introduction of the Sizzler Salad Bar. Whether he received support or even approval from the franchisor to embark on his expanded salad bar project is academic at this point. The fact is, he did and no one could dispute the phenomenal response from the dining out public to his innovation. He didn't just make the salad bar longer. He made it wider and therewith introduced the innovative idea of creating steps or tiers in the crushed ice mounded well above the lip of ice bin. In this way, the number of different items that could be added and attractively displayed expanded geometrically as the length of the bar was extended. Of course, a wider selection of vegetables was added, but to this, for the first time anywhere to my knowledge, we had salad bars with an expansive variety of fruit as well. Plus, we had room for creative mixed salads. And, to cap it off, the ends of the bar were wide enough to add heated foods so on one end he added a selection of soups.

It's safe to say, Jack created a salad bar mania within Sizzler and before long, all sorts of creative things were springing up on Sizzler Salad Bars across the country. In a way, it became a play thing where creativity ran wild. After all, just making a lot of money started to get boring and we had to spend our time doing something.

There was one potential downside risk to the innovative merchandising steps winding its way through Sizzler in the early nineteen-eighties. That being that Sizzler was becoming an increasingly more challenging concept to execute effectively. No one can dispute that it is incumbent on any company producing any product to keep abreast of changing consumer preferences and make appropriate changes in product design to maintain customer loyalty. Staying abreast of the changing tastes and preferences of a company's customers and responding appropriately is probably the central responsibility of the marketing function within a firm. However, the need to meet the changing preferences of customers notwithstanding, from an operations point of view, the three key threats to an ability among the production side of the company to consistently produce a company's product according to design are variety, complexity and change. Thus, what is an elixir for the marketing department— new, different and improved is poison for the operations department.

Certainly, one of the primary responsibilities of senior management within any company is to effectively manage this inherent conflict between the need create new and improved products to meet the changing wants and needs of its customers in a timely fashion and the need among those charged with producing those products to be provided the tools, time and training to respond effectively. To accomplish this, senior management needs to provide itself with some sort of information system by which it can monitor the company's capability to meet this challenge.

To Tom Gregory's great credit, creating this information system was one of his first and probably one of his best contributions to Sizzler. Early in his tenure as President, he presided over a reorganization of the system in which operations oversight, corporate operations support, the development of training systems and top-down communication (and to a lesser degree, bottom-up communication) among corporate stores and franchised stores were merged. This was accomplished by establishing a new department within Sizzler called the System Operations Support Department--S.O.S. for short. The responsibility of the System Operations Support Department was to establish uniform performance standards, develop training systems and materials, and assess each unit's ongoing ability to meet those system performance standards. Sizzler's S.O.S. Department was charged with servicing *all* Sizzlers in the country, franchised and corporate owned alike on an equal basis.

The person put in charge of this department was Walt Fitzgerald. He became Sizzler's first Vice President of System Operations Support. Walt's first priority upon assuming this role was to develop an information feedback system whereby senior management could assess the level of unit performance system wide on a store-by-store basis. To this end, Walt sought the cooperation and support of the opinion leaders among the franchise community by making the development of this information system a joint project of his department and the Board of Trustees of the National Sizzler Franchisee Association.

Walt Fitzgerald's intent was clear. He intended to develop a Unit Performance Audit which would be administered by a cadre of field inspectors. Over the course of about a year involving numerous meetings among his staff and the Trustees the audit form was created. And it was truly a piece of work. It took a Sizzler field inspector anywhere between six to eight hours to conduct an inspection of one unit and complete the form[8].

---

[8] These audits occurred unannounced.

Virtually all aspects of a Sizzler's performance were inspected. Each line item on the inspection list was given a point score. The total points possible varied depending on the perceived degree of importance of a specific performance attribute and the total points possible were two thousand. The total points possible of two thousand never changed however, from time to time the total possible points for any single performance attribute was increased or decreased according to a perceived need to redirect the efforts of unit management.

Another serendipitous outcome of this project was that the creation of an inspection form which measures actual performance against objective standards, forced senior management to more clearly and thoroughly *define* performance standards. Thus, a formerly subjective standard such as taking a customer's order quickly yet efficiently was transformed into the specification that, the average time to take a customer's order, deliver that order to the kitchen and collect that customer's money should be twenty seconds. As another example, providing quality dining room service was transformed into providing seven step service wherein the what, who, how, where and when of each of the required seven steps was clearly defined in a way that was measurable. Moreover, the creation of objective, measurable performance standards greatly enhanced the capability of those responsible to develop employee training systems to communicate what, exactly, constituted proper execution of a specified task.

Not only was the field inspection format well developed, but the way this department was integrated into the organization was also well done. This by virtue of the fact that the S.O.S. Department was placed in the organization's structural hierarchy on an equal level with the corporation's Operations Department with its own Vice President who reported directly to the President. Again, to Tom Gregory's credit, he realized from the beginning that the only way to insure that the field inspection function would provide a truly accurate picture of concept execution, certainly insofar as the inspection of corporate owned units was concerned, was to insulate and protect the inspection staff and its leadership from retribution or politicization by senior operations management which is exactly what would occur in short order if those conducting the inspections reported to those who's operating units they inspected.

Thus, equipped with a field inspection format and a cadre of field inspectors totally disconnected from the Corporate Operations Department, Walt Fitzgerald went to work providing senior management with an ongoing picture of each unit's ability to execute the Sizzler concept according to prescribed standards. Not surprisingly, it quickly became evident that there was a rather wide disparity among the chain's units to execute the concept properly. The first few rounds of inspections, which were administered every three months to every unit in the system, revealed that stores with both the worst performance and the best performance were owned and operated by franchisees. For the most part, the audit scores of corporate owned stores tended to hover in the mid-range.

In the beginning the system wide average score was around 85% with some franchised units earning scores as low as 40% and some as high as 90%. Although the NSFA Trustees all endorsed this program, to Walt Fitzgerald's chagrin, few of them made any attempt to improve the audit scores of their respective units. A high score was great but a low score was no big deal. Walt realized that if the attitude of the thirteen Trustees who, altogether, owned approximately one third of the franchised units in the system, remained relatively casual about the audit scores their units were achieving, the program would not provide much impetus for improvement among the remaining franchisees. But that situation changed dramatically when Walt published the scores of all units in the system in descending score order with the owner of each franchisee and the District Manager of each corporate store also identified. Within months of this innovation, a massive change in the culture of the Sizzler chain began to take place. A genuine concern among all store owners and managers for their audit score swept over the entire restaurant chain and with it, a substantial improvement in system wide concept execution. Moreover, there is no question but that this program was instrumental not only in improving the system's operations performance level, but in causing substantially greater investment in store remodeling projects throughout the nineteen-eighties than probably would have occurred in its absence

From the time Sizzler began publishing unit audit scores until the S.O.S. Department was dismantled in nineteen ninety-five, a desire to achieve a high score was almost as important among most franchisees and corporate District Managers as a desire to achieve satisfactory sales levels. Few within the Sizzler system would argue today that Sizzler's unit evaluation program did not play a vital role in the chain's ability to grow and prosper throughout the nineteen-eighties.[9]

And grow and prosper it did--for all the reasons described. In nineteen eighty a total of 452 Sizzlers were in operation comprised of 128 corporate units and 324 franchised units. System wide sales were two hundred fifty-nine million dollars and per store average annual sales were five hundred seventy-three thousand dollars. By nineteen ninety, the number of corporate owned stores had increased to 209 and there were 455 franchised stores in the system making a total of 664 operating Sizzlers. System wide sales were just under nine hundred seventeen million dollars and per store average sales were a million three hundred eighty-five thousand dollars.

If Sizzler stock holders were pleased, then one could surmise that Sizzler franchisees were ecstatic. By this time, I owned four Sizzlers in Sonoma County California and altogether these four units were generating almost eight million dollars a year in gross sales. Annual discretionary cash flow from my company's store level operations i.e., pre-

---

[9] Most of the time, the Sizzlers I owned earned audit scores in the top 20% of the rankings. On a few occasions, one of my units managed to be ranked Number One in the Nation. During one round of the quarterly evaluation process in the mid-nineteen-eighties, the four Sizzlers I owned at that time were ranked First, Second, Third and Fifth in Performance Excellence among all Sizzlers in the United States.

tax profit plus depreciation exceeded one million dollars. To say times were good would be an understatement. Times were fabulous. All of us in Sizzler, corporate management and franchisees alike, considered ourselves invincible. We believed we were dialed into a money-making program that would make all of us very wealthy. As Sizzler entered the last decade of the century, plans for further expansion continued unabated. The company's nineteen ninety Annual Report, dated April 30th 1990 indicated corporate plans to open new units at the rate of ten to twenty a year with expectations that somewhere between sixty-five and seventy-five additional franchised units would open annually. I fully expected to build more units in the nineteen-nineties and therewith pile more cash on top of the million dollars a year my four stores were generating at that time.

But, alas, this was not to be. The fate that awaited the Sizzler restaurant chain and those of us who had invested our money and careers in it would turn out to be something entirely different. It was a fate none of us in the Sizzler organization, not in our wildest dreams--or should I say nightmares could have imagined. The following charts tell the story:

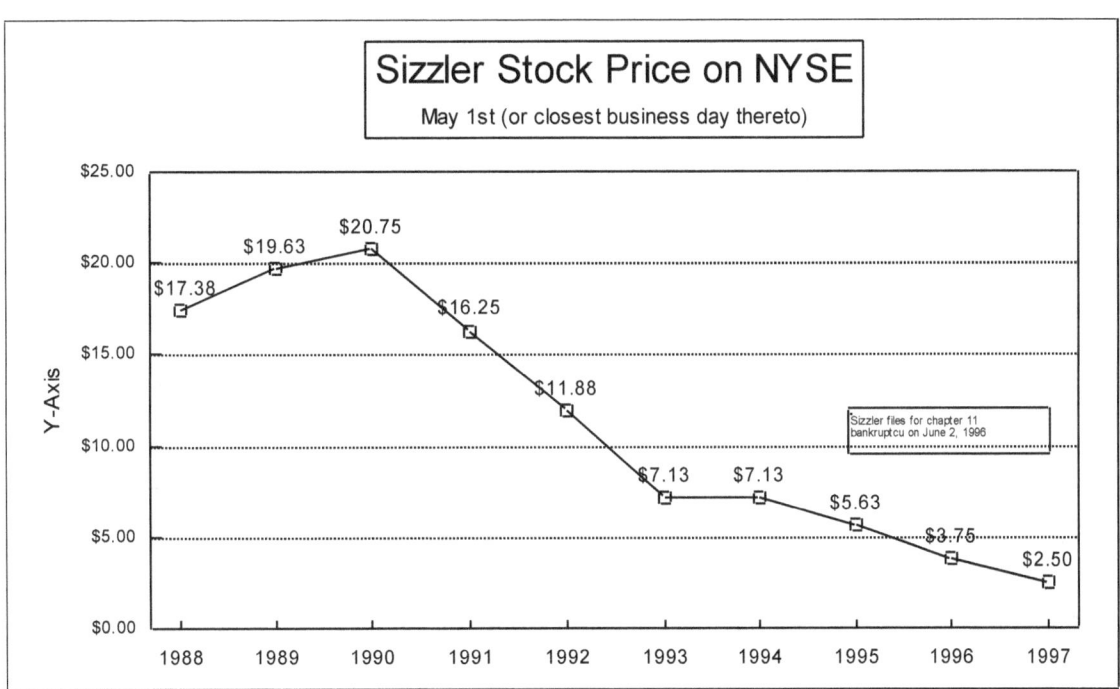

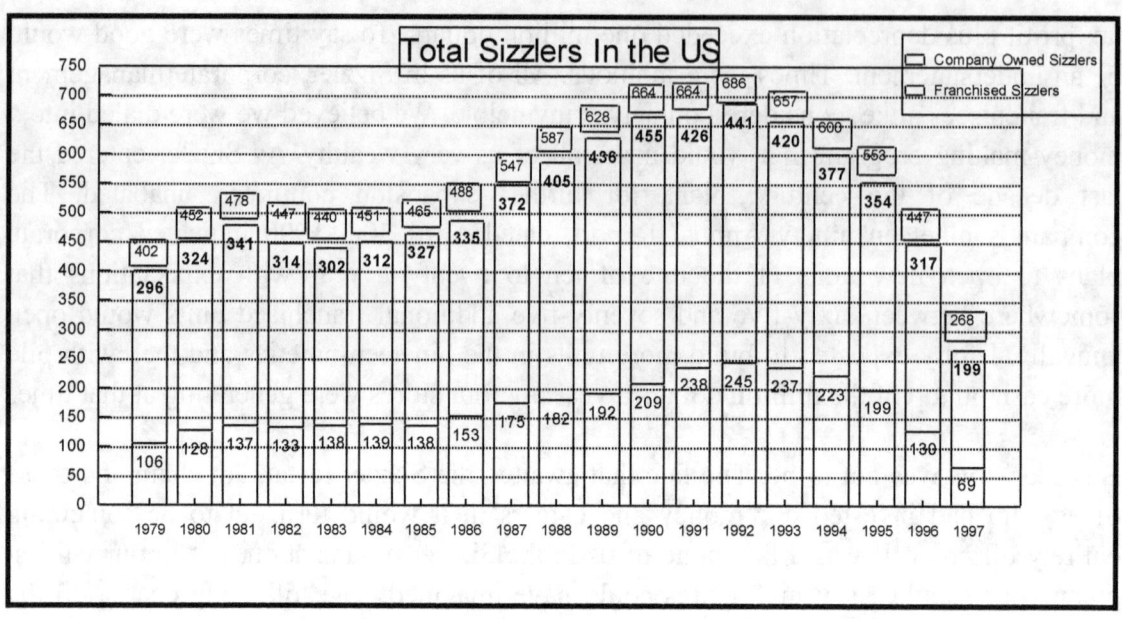

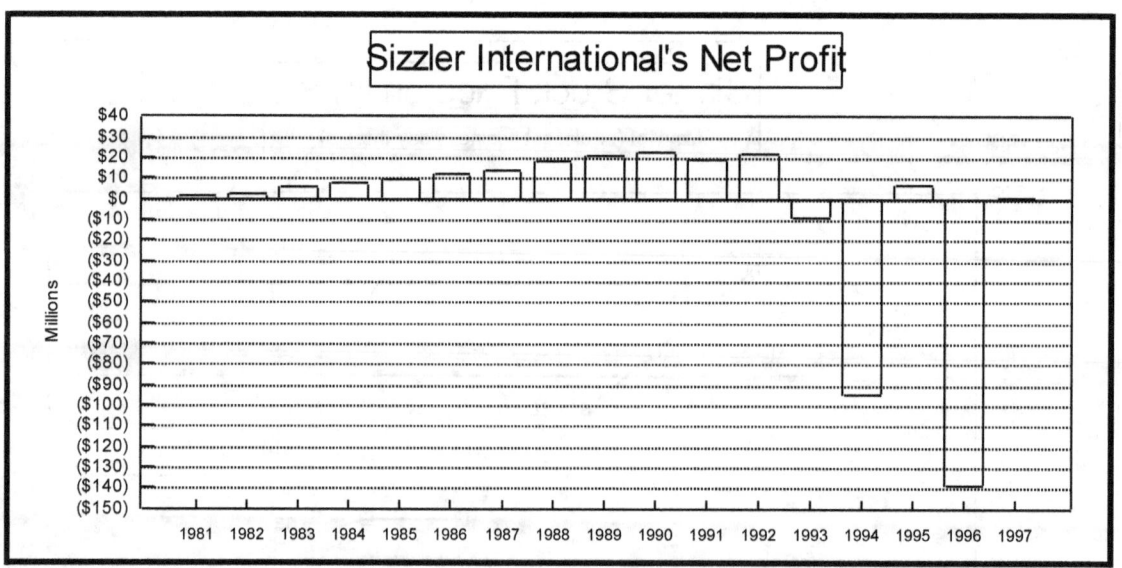

What happened that could have undermined one of the country's strongest regional restaurant chains so quickly and so thoroughly?

Chapter 3
The Decline of Sizzler

Beginning in the late nineteen-seventies through the early nineteen-nineties every other year, Sizzler Restaurants International would hold a national convention at which all senior management, and much of the company's middle management plus all Franchisees and BBDO's Sizzler Account staff would attend. On the in-between years, the Sizzler National Franchisee Association would host a Sizzler Conference to which all franchisees, senior Sizzler management and the advertising agency staff was invited. In 1989 the NSFA held its biannual conference in New Orleans. One of the key topics of discussion at this conference was Sizzler management's idea of further expanding the Sizzler Salad Bar by surrounding it with satellite bars such as a Desert Bar, a Past Bar, a Tostada Bar and a Hot Appetizer Bar. Part and parcel with the introduction of these additional food bars would be an advertising campaign wherein Sizzler would introduce this array as Sizzler's new Buffet Court.

Sizzler's top management were solidly behind the Buffet Court idea and their mission in New Orleans was to persuade the franchisees to get behind it also. Growth in per store average sales, although still upward, was slowing down and management was eager to try something that would rekindle the kind of sales increases that we had enjoyed in prior years. The logic behind the Buffet Court being that Sizzler could thereby develop a more compelling appeal to the all-you-can-eat market segment, a segment toward which Sizzler had moved steadily in the second half of the decade with Steak and All You Can Eat Shrimp and All you Can Eat Barbecued Beef Bones.

To senior Sizzler management's dismay, the Buffet Court idea was not well received by everyone. Perhaps a third of Sizzler's franchisees were strongly opposed to the idea, a third were sitting on the fence and a third were what can best be described as open minded. The principal opposition to the idea--even among the open-minded franchisees--was that this idea represented a significant departure from Sizzler's proven format. The biggest concern being that such an innovation could change people's perception of Sizzler as a budget steak house which is what Sizzler still was, the Salad Bar notwithstanding into a buffet restaurant. There was also some concern regarding the system's capability to effectively execute this idea given the existing configuration and limitations of our physical facilities.

These concerns among the franchisee community are well documented. At this time, I was the Writer, Editor and Publisher of *The Catalyst*, the official National Sizzler Franchisee Association News Letter. In this capacity, I interviewed Mike Minchin regarding the franchisees' objections and worries. Following is the full text of this interview conducted in December 1989 as it appeared in the Volume 2, Number 1 Spring 1990 edition of *The Catalyst*.

THE CATALYST INTERVIEW: MIKE MINCHIN

a candid conversation with the Executive Vice President of SRI about the evolution of the Sizzler Salad Bar into the Sizzler Buffet Court.

By early spring of 1989, franchisees were hearing rumors that SRI was heavily involved in testing an "exponential" increase in Salad Bar products. There was talk of hot appetizers, soft serve ice cream and even deli sandwiches being tested for inclusion. Mike Minchin was overheard to say he was thinking not simply of enlarging the existing salad bar to accommodate these products but of adding entirely new bars alongside what currently exists; "a veritable 'Disneyland of bars'" to use his words.

To say that these tests were regarded by many with skepticism is an understatement. Speculation was rife that Mike Minchin had lost his mind. Few seemed convinced SIZZLER was staying on the right road.

Nevertheless, the rumors persisted. So did the speculation about Minchin's mental health and Sizzler's direction. By summer the rumors were being confirmed as true. A metamorphosis of the salad bar into a "food bar" was well under way in Sizzler's Atlanta market, Mike Macatte and Bob Harrod's Louisville market and at selected sites in the Los Angeles area.[10]

At the NSFA conference in New Orleans in November 1989, speculation was put to and end by presentations from Mike Minchin and Jim McGinnis confirming that SRI was committed to changing our system's current Salad Bar concept into a "Buffet Court." This announcement immediately raised a plethora of questions among franchisees, some of which were answered and some of which were not.

*In an effort to gain greater clarification on this new and important issue, **The Catalyst** contacted Mike Minchin at his executive suite as SRI World Headquarters in Los Angeles in December. Following is the result of that meeting.*

CATALYST: Why go to the Buffet Court at all? What's wrong with just continuing to do what we are doing now?

MINCHIN: We could continue with what we are doing now because we are already a Buffet Court--with our Tostada Bar, Soup Bar, Salad Bar, Muffin Bar, etc. The term Buffet Court appropriately and uniquely captures the nature of our current bar set-up. Yet it more appropriately captures the breadth of our bars rather than referring to them

---

[10] Mike Macatte, a former Vice President of Operations for Sizzler International and Bob Harrod were franchisees who, in partnership developed the Louisville, Kentucky area.

collectively as Salad Bar. We are suggesting the addition of one to three new sales generating bars--the Appetizer Bar, the Dessert Bar and the Deli Bar. In some areas of the country, we need to add these bars in order to remain competitive. In other parts it is a unique opportunity to generate significant incremental sales, bring or return a higher value image to Sizzler, and to add real needed news...especially to those areas where competition has tended to make our concept appear ho-hum.

CATALYST: Do you view the introduction of the Buffet Court as a new re-positioning for Sizzler? If so, what new market niche are we moving into and what niche are we leaving?

MINCHIN: I don't think of it as a new repositioning, but rather a natural evolution designed to meet changing customer needs. For example, the feature article in a recent *Nation's Restaurant News* talked about the trend to appetizers as a main meal. We still are a casual, contemporary, popular priced restaurant offering a wide variety of good wholesome foods in an easy, convenient manner. If anything, the addition of these three new bars should broaden our appeal, especially during any economic downturn.

CATALYST: Is the Buffet Court just another marketing department test or is it a *fait accompli*?

MINCHIN: It is a test in that we are continuing to gather specific information about the impact of these bars on food costs, sales and profitability. At the same time, we are rolling it out in key markets, both for defensive and offensive reasons. Also, we want to control this roll-out, therefore we have requested any franchisee to get prior approval for its installation. In this manner we can carefully manage its use; update everyone on any new information. Since controlling food costs is an essential part of this roll-out, we need to exert extra efforts to ensure that we are purchasing the approved items, thereby guaranteeing maximum discounts. No longer does the competitive environment, or economic conditions permit the longer testing and roll-out of products experienced in the past. I guess, in summary, you can say this project falls somewhere between a test and a *fait accompli*--or a test-accompli!

CATALYST: What can franchisees anticipate in terms of sales increases, labor and food cost increases, change in check average, change in customer counts and change in bottom line results once the Buffet Court is installed?

MINCHIN: In our test units, sales have increased from 9.5% to as much as 30% with no additions other that the Buffet Court. Overall check averages are down anywhere from .7% to a maximum of 5.7%. With the addition of the Buffet Court, lunch check average remains about the same. Dinner is lower due to some trade-over. In direct proportion to sales, customer counts are up 9% to 33%. Labor stays flat, or in some instances went down 1% to 2%.

CATALYST: Is SRI going to install the Buffet Court in all company-owned Sizzlers? If so or if not, how will this impact your high-volume stores?

MINCHIN: If the Buffet Court continues to generate its presently indicated favorable results, we, in concert with franchisees in mixed markets, would like to move forward throughout the Spring-Summer seasons of nineteen ninety.

CATALYST: What storing, cooking, holding and serving equipment must be added to the back of the house to support the Buffet Court and where is there room to install it? Do you anticipate any special problems retrofitting additional fryers and requisite exhaust hoods?

MINCHIN: All of the company units have installed a henny-penny type holding cabinet in the back of the house to sandbag some of the appetizer and dessert items. Our hot sides don't leave much room for expansion, but in a few instances, we've been able to remove two existing electric fryers and replace them with three gas units which have a much shorter recovery time. The small wares package of ice cream dishes, 1/3 and 1/2 pans, will run an additional $3,000. The majority of the Buffet Court items are frozen. You might find it necessary to add a Traulson type two door freezer along one of your back walls. To date, none of our mid image or mew image units have found it unmanageable.

CATALYST: Can the franchisees expect Sizzler Operations Support to be ready to affect a timely delivery of Buffet Court related training materials, recipes, product specifications, etc.?

MINCHIN: It would be our objective, as always, to have Sizzler Operations ready to support the entire system in the roll-out of these new bars.

CATALYST: Are you concerned the Buffet Court may be just a fad that will lose the customer's interest as fast as it appears to be captured?

MINCHIN: I do not believe that the three bars are a fad. Ice cream is and continues to be America's favorite dessert. It is too fundamental to our culture to quickly pass. Unless for some crazy reason we find it causes cancer. Hot cobblers continue to be a favorite since mom's time and before. the appetizer bar is filled with long-term favorites, from macaroni and cheese to popular fried vegetables and finger foods like fired chicken which for years in many restaurants people have paid $3.00--$5.00 for a serving. A good deli sandwich must go back to Moses' day. The three bars constitute exciting new offerings of broadly popular basic American foods. Results to date show no fall-off in popularity and I'd be surprised it will. Of course, from time to time, we might want to substitute items, for example scallop potatoes for macaroni and cheese, pizza for pasta, etcetera to add even more interest. We've been testing the full Buffet Court in Louisville now for over three years and consumer interest continues strong.[11] Furthermore, the exciting thing about the Buffet Court is that it opens up an entire new area of new product opportunity, one which sometimes our limited space and abilities on the hot side do not permit. For instance, the pasta bar can be easily converted to an Italian Bar serving pizza, meatballs in marinara sauce and spaghetti. The appetizer bar at lunch could be converted to a make-your-own-French-dip-sandwich bar. Wow, my mind is full of exciting possibilities to keep our concept fresh, strong and exciting to our customers and these new bars open up a whole new arena.

CATALYST: Is there any concern at SRI that with the introduction of the Buffet Court you are creating a Sizzler that is just too complex to effectively manage?

MINCHIN: It is always my concern about moving too fast or making our concept too complex to manage. I recognize that it is substantially more difficult that it was in the seventies. But at the same time, it is substantially more successful. We just cannot stand still. Will Rogers said, "Even if you're on the right track, you'll get run over if you sit there." Current experience with these three new bars, while requiring new learning, see to be well within our abilities to handle.

CATALYST: Are there any plans afoot to reduce the advertising contribution that ad coop members must make once the Buffet Court has been rolled out market wide?

MINCHIN: It would be my judgment that the move to the Buffet Court & Grill is the kind of exciting news one would *want* to advertise. It is a unique opportunity to rebuild the value perception of Sizzler, both among current and prospective customers. However, if a choice had to be made between no Buffet Court and advertising as contrasted with a Buffet Court and lesser advertising...I'd go for the latter. Put the value on the customer's plate vs. into the airwaves. It has proven to accelerate sales by word of mouth alone...which in the end is the best kind of advertising.

CATALYST: When can franchises get an approval to install a Buffet Court?

MINCHIN: Franchisees can get approval to install a Buffet Court by writing me why they feel it is needed. Also, we are requiring at this time an evaluation of 90+.

CATALYST: What advice can you offer franchisees *vis-à-vis* the Buffet Court who are now in the process of remodeling a store or building a new one?

MINCHIN: It would be my strong recommendation to any franchisee remodeling a store or building a new one to plan for its construction.

---

[11] The franchise owner/operators of all the Sizzlers in Louisville eventually filed for chapter 7 Liquidation Bankruptcy. In hindsight, I think the performance data they were supplying SRI may not have been entirely accurate.

CATALYST: Are you concerned that Sizzler's competitors will quickly follow our lead with a Buffet Court of their own and significantly negate our anticipated benefits?

MINCHIN: I can't be concerned with what our competitors do in copying us. They have done it all throughout the eighties. That's the price of leadership. I believe our food court arrangement of bars (as contrasted with food troughs) and our quality of product and operations, all together give us a substantial advantage; one which is difficult for them to copy. Furthermore, I have strong confidence in our ability to stay ahead with new ideas.

CATALYST: How upbeat are you about the Buffet Court concept?

MINCHIN: I believe the new, Sizzler Buffet Court and Grill positioning with the three new bars, is the most dramatic and positive move forward since our initial repositioning in the early eighties. Both Tom Gregory and I are strongly in agreement on this.

In retrospect, it is easy to see now that the franchisees' concerns were prophetic. They proved to be well founded and today, there is no question but that the introduction of the Buffet Court was the beginning of the end for Sizzler. Of course, hind sight is always twenty-twenty. In the fall of nineteen eighty-nine, without benefit of a crystal ball, all we could see were that sales were starting to go flat and, in some cases, actually decline and, we guessed, competition from various buffet restaurants springing up across the country were probably responsible, in part, for this dilemma. We knew, or at least senior Sizzler management made clear that they had to do something. Just accepting a declining sales trend was never considered as a viable alternative.

Although senior Sizzler management sought the endorsement of the Trustees of the National Sizzler Franchisee Association for their Buffet Court idea in New Orleans all they came away with was an endorsement of a commitment on the part of Sizzler to thoroughly test market the idea before making a system-wide commitment to it. This was a wise and reasonable position for the Trustees to take and should have been Sizzler's strategy in the first place.

With that endorsement in hand, the NSFA conference closed on a peaceful note and Sizzler management returned to Los Angeles to begin testing the Buffet Court. The agreement was that the company would convert six corporate stores, three in Southern California and three in the San Francisco Bay Area, to the Buffet Court concept and carefully observe performance results for at least six months or longer if necessary.

Sometime late in nineteen eighty-nine Sizzler had completed its conversion of the six test stores to the Buffet Court concept and it was off to the races so to speak. However, in late Spring, nineteen ninety, a major announcement came forth from Sizzler Headquarters in Los Angeles. That being that customers were extraordinarily positively responsive to the Buffet Court and that sales, by this time starting to show signs of an actual decline system wide--for the first time in Sizzler's history--were climbing back up in the test stores. With that, the testing of the Buffet Court was declared an unequivocal success and all corporate owned stores would be retrofitted with Buffet Courts according to Dick Birmingham "as fast as humanly possible." Moreover, all new television commercials to be developed by BBDO would prominently feature the Buffet Court.

The decision to produce a new genre of TV commercials featuring the Buffet Court and removing all others from the system has a significance beyond the obvious. Keep in mind that by this time the Sizzler system, corporate and franchised stores alike, were as dependent on constant doses of TV advertising as a heroin addict is on *his* drug of choice. Thus, in the major markets where corporate stores comprised the greatest number of Sizzlers, which would be all regions of California, Arizona, Florida, Atlanta and the North Eastern United States, a franchisee had no real option but to offer the products advertised on television or face a major defection of his customers. For better or for worse, the introduction of the Buffet Court was to become Sizzler's new marketing strategy whether the franchisees agreed or not.

System wide, several million dollars were invested by Sizzler Restaurants International and its franchisees installing the various satellite bars. This also necessitated the elimination of many tables in the dining room as well--effectively making our restaurants smaller and thereby requiring that each seat in the dining room support a larger burden of fixed costs. However, true to prediction, sales increased with the introduction of the Buffet Court--for a while. What we discovered, much to our dismay, was that these satellite bars were regarded by many of our current customers as a novelty that they all had to try at least once or twice. After the novelty appeal of the Buffet Court wore off, realty set in.

The realty being that to purchase a steak dinner or other entree *and* the Buffet Court was too much food and too costly. The option of purchasing an entree and a Salad Bar was no longer available. This fact turned off many of our loyal steak and salad customers and they went elsewhere. Within less than a year, Sizzler lost a large number of its formally loyal budget steak customers and Salad Bar customers and the erosion of this market segment has continued unabated ever since. To some degree these departing customers were replaced by people for whom an all-you-can-eat buffet dining experience had an appeal. However. the offset to the departing budget steak customer provided by the new market segment didn't make up for the customers we lost. Moreover, there is a limit to how much a restaurant can charge for an all-you-can-eat buffet and it was less than what we were charging for our entrees. Thus, Sizzler not only suffered a declining customer

33

base, but a declining average check as well which meant a decline in its average gross margin per customer. Per store average sales began to decline and unit profits began to plummet. Within two years of the introduction of the Buffet Court, close to seventy percent of Sizzler's customers were only purchasing the Buffet Court.

Although it was never intended that Sizzler would reposition itself as a Buffet Restaurant in the market place and simultaneously abandon its position as a Budget Family Steak House chain, that's exactly what it accomplished. In so doing, it created many other problems for itself. First of all, the economics of Buffet Restaurants are fundamentally different from those for a steak house. Buffet Restaurants typically feature very large dining rooms that can accommodate upwards of three hundred guests or more at a time, yet can do so with an occupancy cost which, on a per square foot basis or per dining room seat basis, is relatively low compared to a Sizzler. The need for greater seating capacity is due partly to the fact that somewhat more time is required, on the average, for people to indulge in a buffet dining event relative a cook-to-order dining event. Thus, it requires more dining room seats to serve an equal number of people during peak meal times in a buffet restaurant. Considering all the remodeling that had occurred in the nineteen-eighties and the expensive new units being built, coupled with the reduction in seating to accommodate the satellite bars, the occupancy cost per square foot or per seat for a Sizzler was well above that of other buffet restaurants. Sizzler had managed to reposition itself into a market niche for which its existing occupancy costs per dining room seat were too high relative to other buffet concepts. Moreover, the new Buffet Restaurant competition that began to appear across the country were offering a variety of food selections within their larger dining rooms with which Sizzler simply could not compete. Thus, Sizzler had managed to reposition itself into a market niche for which its physical facilities were too small, improperly laid out and too expensive to compete effectively.

This mistake was further compounded, I believe, by Sizzler's very gradual shift in its entree menu pricing policy beginning in the mid nineteen-seventies. In the company's early years, a Sizzler Restaurant's *Cost of Goods Sold* hovered in the mid to high 40% range--approximately 45%. This means that the company was multiplying a particular entree's cost of raw materials by something between 2.1 and 2.5 times to arrive at the retail price.[12] Over the years, Sizzler began using an ever-higher markup multiplier on its entrees. At the time of the Buffet Court's introduction, the markup multiplier used on Sizzler's hamburgers, steak, seafood plates and all menu entrees generally (excluding items promoted on TV and price reductions created by discount coupons) was in the neighborhood of *3 to 4 times cost.* Thus, over the years, Sizzler's entree cost markup pricing policy had increased by more than 60% and for some steak entrees it had

---

[12] Actually, this is an average markup multiplier. A detailed analysis of each menu item would reveal that the entree itself was marked up maybe 2.0 or 2.2 times its cost while beverages and salads were marked up by anywhere from 3 to 5 times their cost yielding an overall or average markup of 2.5 times cost.

increased by 100%. We were able to get away with this due to the buoyant economic condition prevalent through most of the nineteen-eighties coupled with Sizzler's powerful advertising presence. Nevertheless, I think the long-term effect on the consuming public's perception of Sizzler brought about by this evolution in Sizzler's pricing policy was an erosion or degradation in the credibility of the chain's efforts to remain positioned as a Budget Steak House and to compete effectively with other budget steak houses—especially in the South East. Moreover, my criticism of Sizzler senior management notwithstanding, this is the one factor in Sizzler's decline where the franchisees generally and the franchisee leadership in particular, namely the Board of Trustees of NSFA—including myself--must bear much of the blame.

With one exception, there was never a voice for moderation in our aggressive pricing practices; never a concern for the long-term risks of using an ever-increasing cost mark-up multiplier to set retail prices. Indeed, there was not even much of an awareness for the ever so gradual but always upward drift in our pricing policy and certainly there was no awareness for how far we had drifted. We were living for the moment, basking in the glow of strong consumer acceptance we believed would be ours forever. The one exception to this short sightedness among the franchisees was Vince Liuzza. As early as nineteen eighty and intermittently thereafter he made repeated attempts to alert Sizzler management and its franchisees to the problem. In letters and in open discussion at Sizzler conventions and assorted other get-togethers Vince warned repeatedly that Sizzler's success on TV was camouflaging a fundamental and debilitating weakness in the system's inability to compete on price and value with most of Sizzler's main competitors. As Vince tried to point out, Sizzler had to either temper its aggressive pricing policy or modify its budget steak image to one where the higher prices would make sense. But, alas, no one would listen. As early as nineteen eighty-three Vince Liuzza warned senior management that this ill-considered propensity to over price our entrees would eventually cause as much damage to the Sizzlers in California as it was then causing in Louisiana and when that happened, it would be the end for Sizzler. Prophets are typically without honor in their own house.

With the introduction of the Buffet Court, other operational problems began to crop up for Sizzler as well. If seventy percent of Sizzler's customers were selecting the Buffet Court as their entree, then obviously, only thirty percent were ordering off the traditional entree menu. Eventual efforts to reverse the trend in consumer purchasing behavior back toward the entree menu became focused on creating new products to feature. This resulted in a proliferation of entree selections to an already crowded menu and by simple division one can surmise that not very many of any single product offered on the traditional menu were purchased on any given day. Thus, both the requisite skill needed to produce each product which comes with production repetition and the freshness of the raw ingredients declined. Sometimes a day or two would go by in any given Sizzler where no one ordered a particular entree offered for sale. To say that Sizzler served fresh fish really came to mean only that Sizzler purchased fresh fish. What it served on occasion was an altogether different story.

In addition to this problem, it brought about a further degradation in Sizzler's ability to keep hourly employee training systems current. This was a constant problem for Sizzler due to the never-ending propensity to tweak the system in one small way or another throughout its history. Although Sizzler devoted a lot of attention to various audio-visual and printed hourly employee training delivery systems, I do not believe the training material delivered thereby was *ever* in total synchronization with what was currently being advocated as the proper way to perform all tasks and prepare all products. Of course, this situation only got worse with the introduction of the Buffet Court.

Plus, given the large number of products required to stock the Buffet Court in addition to Sizzler's expansive entree menu, product storage also became a big problem. In theory, a store manager had only to purchase less of any particular product as demand for that product declined and therefore, available storage space should not be an issue. As a practical matter, however, to maintain food cost at an acceptable level, the ingredients and products a unit purchased had to be purchased in bulk quantity. Add to this the general fear among managers of running out of some menu item due to the often-unmerciful haranguing customers like to bestow on a restaurant staff when the place is out of something they want and the result is a chaotic product storage situation.

As problems go, the cramped storage and resulting improper storage, rotation and handling of raw ingredients in the pantry, storage shelves, refrigerators and freezers may seem rather mild. However, possibly as a result of this problem, one of the single greatest blows to Sizzler's reputation occurred. In April nineteen ninety-three a news story hit the Associated Press Wire and was reported on all the major networks in the U.S. and via Turner Broadcasting, throughout the world. Ten people fell ill after contracting E. coli food poisoning at two Sizzlers in Grants Pass and North Bend, Oregon. This was perceived by the news media as a major event due to the fact that three months earlier two hundred people had ingested the heretofore unfamiliar E. coli at a large number of Jack-in-the-Boxes in Seattle Washington and caused one death. Thus, the country had a new major health threat and Sizzler was portrayed as the second restaurant in the country guilty of infecting people with it.[13]

The fact is that E. coli has been around since before recorded history however, the existence of the particularly savage E. coli 0157:H7 strain has only been known to scientists for about fourteen years. Thus, it's unlikely that Sizzler was only the second restaurant which caused such an infection. However, the existence of E. coli and the people who contracted this bacterium were of no interest to the news media prior to the

---

[13] According to ABC News (6 pm PST 8/16/97) it is estimated that approximately 20,000 Americans a year become infected by this bacterium.

Jack-in-the-Box incident. Moreover, in Sizzler's case, the event was limited to two franchised restaurants where there were only ten confirmed victims, none of whom died. Unlike Jack-in-the-Box which caused a wide spread outbreak among customers in many of its units, the Sizzler incident was more of a random unfortunate chance event.

Indeed, the simultaneous investigations into the cause launched by Sizzler Restaurants International and Oregon State Health Officials concluded that although cattle are the only source of the E. coli bacteria, the consumption of beef was *not* the cause of this incident. The conclusion of these investigations was that the source of the contamination was from *mayonnaise* or some product(s) which included mayonnaise such as salad dressing or coleslaw. The only way this could be possible would be from cross-contamination meaning that the blood and juices in raw meat somehow managed to seep into the mayonnaise or mayonnaise-based products. How this occurred was never determined. Oregon's State Health Officials said that their inspection of both Sizzlers revealed the restaurants had sound food handling practices and would not be required to close.[14]

Given the fact that there was a simultaneous outbreak of E. coli food poisoning in two Sizzlers, Dr. Katrina Hedberg, Deputy State Epidemiologist, theorized that the cross contamination may have occurred during truck transport where a leak developed in the packages holding the raw beef and in this manner, the juices dripped down through the twist-tie seal on a couple of containers of bulk mayonnaise which was stored in close proximity to the beef.[15] Subsequently, the Grants Pass Sizzler got one of the contaminated cartons of mayonnaise the North Bend Sizzler got the other. Although never proven, the theory seems plausible and if this was indeed the cause, then Sizzler was also an innocent victim of this freak accident and nothing more.

Nonetheless, the media had a field day at Sizzler's expense and this only accelerated Sizzler's decline.

To Sizzler's credit, senior management reacted strongly to this incident by requiring that all store managers as well as all corporate operations management at all levels and all franchisees go through a three-day formal training program on proper food handling procedures. In addition, Sizzler instituted a vigorous program to improve food storage and handling procedures throughout the system. This fact, of course, was never reported by the media. However, always watchful for an opportunity to ruin someone, the media pounced on Sizzler a second time when it learned through a health department announcement that another Sizzler in Seattle Washington had caused a second outbreak of e. coli. This was disastrous for Sizzler, and to add insult to injury, after months of

---

[14] Nation's Restaurant News, April 19, 1993 Volume 27, No. 3, p. 3

[15] *Ibid.*

investigation by experts in an attempt to identify the specific cause of the second e. coli incident, the conclusion was that the local health department had made a mistake. The Sizzler, in fact, was not the cause of a recent e. coli outbreak in the community. Neither was this bit of news reported by the media.

Another problem brought on by the Buffet Court was the exacerbation of a challenge with which Sizzler unit managers had to cope since the inception of the salad bar. This was the frustration of dealing with customers who would help themselves to the Buffet Court without having paid for it. There is a fundamental incompatibility in offering an All-You-Can-Eat salad bar or buffet dining experience within the same dining room where cook-to-order entrees are featured. The problem comes up when customers who order off the cook-to-order menu and do not also purchase the right to visit the Buffet Court help themselves to it anyway. This propensity for customers to consume food for which they have not paid ranged from very minor incidents of picking a few tidbits off the plate of another person in their party to flagrant abuse by re-using the plate of another person in their party to make an entire additional free meal for themselves.

Sizzler addressed this problem by posting no sharing signs on the menu and on the Salad Bar Sneeze Guard and by such other means as offering a lower priced One-Trip to the Buffet Court opportunity to those purchasing a cook-to-order entree. These attempts to minimize the problem did work to some degree but were not perfect. The problem of sharing persisted nevertheless. Ultimately, it was left up to the unit management staff to try to keep the sharing problem under control as best he or she could. This requirement created an enormous problem for Sizzler which I am not sure senior management ever fully appreciated. That is that part of the unit level management's job description became one of acting as Salad Bar Police. Depending upon the personality of a particular manager and depending upon how much pressure was placed on that individual by his or her superiors to keep food cost under control, the vigor with which store managers carried out their policeman responsibilities ranged from passive acceptance of the problem to actions that went way beyond what was reasonable or appropriate.

For example, after leaving the Sizzler organization, I had a chance conversation with Ginger Elliott in Reno, Nevada. She could vividly recount her last visit to a Sizzler. "Before my dad died," Ginger told me, "he and my mom went to the Sizzler all the time. It was my dad's favorite restaurant. My dad had to go to Sizzler even on vacation whether we were in Hawaii, New Orleans or Florida. During one of my visits back home to San Diego, I took my mom to the Sizzler where she and my dad used to go. She ordered Malibu Chicken and I had the Buffet Court. As we were eating lunch, she picked a couple of vegetables from my plate. The store manager saw this and really told my mom off for doing what she had done."

"My mother was so embarrassed by this encounter," Ginger recalled, "that she started to cry. This upset me so much I couldn't eat; neither could my mom. A few minutes after this confrontation, we both left and neither she nor I have gone back to a Sizzler since."

One can imagine the thousands upon thousands of negative impressions of Sizzler this activity created in the minds of Sizzler's guests over the years. The unit managers were given a no-win task they had to repeatedly perform day in and day out for which no truly effective training, formal system-wide policy or merchandising tactics were ever developed to solve this problem completely. It may well be that there was no solution to this problem other than including the right to visit the Buffet Court with every meal-- which would be cost prohibitive--or eliminating the Buffet Court altogether.

Thus, Sizzler sank deeper and deeper into a slump. Yet, at this early date in its decline, the company was still a strong competitor in most of its markets. When Sizzler embarked on the Buffet Court marketing strategy, the number of operating units across the country were at an all-time high, sales were still reasonably strong and the money available for advertising was flowing nearly as strong as ever. Given Sizzler's television advertising muscle in its major regional markets, it could sell anything. Sizzler encouraged people in large numbers to come in and try the Buffet Court. The public responded to this invitation as enthusiastically as it responded to Sizzler's advertising for many years. However, in this case, much of the public didn't like the experience and didn't like it so much that they stopped going to Sizzler. The result was that the money available to draw people in to try the Buffet Court, was no longer available to try to steer the customer in a new direction once Sizzler realized the mistake it had made. This advertising capability turned out to be a one-way street.

One idea that occurred early on was to simply put things back the way they were. That is, remove the satellite bars, get rid of the high-cost hot appetizers, lower the price of the salad bar and refocus on selling steak. A few franchisees tried this strategy and, in every case, the outcome was an unmitigated disaster. It was easy to get rid of the Buffet Court and many of the customers who came to Sizzler for that reason. That could pretty much be accomplished overnight. However, getting the budget steak customer to come back was an entirely different matter. Once Sizzler had repositioned itself in the dining out public's mind as a Buffet Restaurant, changing the perception of a sufficiently large segment of the population back to being a steak house proved to be impossible. In the few instances where this was tried, customer counts and sales dropped drastically, and the unit became doomed to certain failure. Sizzler had literally steered itself up the proverbial effluent creek and then lost the paddle.

By nineteen ninety-three in every regional market where Sizzler operated, the capability to generate the advertising dollars necessary to maintain a continuous presence on television had been lost. In some of its smaller markets populated only by franchised units--Albuquerque for example--this capability had been lost several years earlier. Once

Sizzler lost its greatest competitive advantage, the ability of a whole new list of competitors such as Applebees, Chili's, Red Lobster, Olive Garden, Hometown Buffet, Golden Corral, and a host of others had a field day taking bites out of Sizzler's customer base.

Chapter 4
Post hoc ergo proctor hoc

*P*ost hoc ergo proctor hoc is a Latin term describing a common error in logical deduction. It means, after this, therefore because of this. In Sizzler's case the popular conclusion for the chain's decline was the introduction of the Buffet Court for all the reasons described in the preceding chapter. However, the Buffet Court fiasco was really only a symptom of the underlying problems that plagued Sizzler.

Simply blaming Sizzler's troubles on the Buffet Court and leaving it at that leaves unanswered many questions about senior management's role in precipitating the situation. After all, the Buffet Court, in and of itself, is nothing more than an inanimate bundle of wood, metal, tile and glass. The real cause of Sizzler's troubles, in the final analysis, lie in the actions, attitudes, behavior, perceptions, decisions and policies of Sizzler's senior management.

Sizzler's Buffet Court Repositioning was implemented in nineteen ninety. This was a watershed year for Sizzler Restaurants International. The company's Annual Report for fiscal nineteen ninety which ended on April 30th, 1990 includes two statements which, considered in retrospect identify the point at which the restaurant chain reached its peak. The report announces that fiscal nineteen ninety marked the ninth consecutive year of record sales and profits for the chain and that the central element of its plan to extend this trend into the next decade was the Buffet Court. Clearly, nineteen ninety was the beginning of the end for Sizzler even though system wide sales continued upward for two more years, breaking the Billion Dollar mark in nineteen ninety and peaking at $1,121,400,000 in nineteen ninety-two.

As I shall point out in the next chapter, much of the reason for Sizzler's decline can be attributed to events that occurred beginning in nineteen ninety-two. However, I believe there were many underlying causes for the chain's collapse that were rooted in circumstances that preceded the last decade of the century. We shall explore those reasons in this chapter.

Christopher Thomas, Sizzler's Chief Financial Officer was interviewed on television in Los Angeles by Grieg Patterson, host of the Dow Jones Investor Network on August 8th, 1996. As Chris Thomas explained on this program, one of the main reasons Sizzler filed for Chapter 11 Bankruptcy protection was a tactical maneuver to rid the company of approximately one hundred thirty underperforming restaurants. In a nutshell, what Chris meant by this was that Sizzler filed Chapter 11 as a means by which to break approximately one hundred thirty long term lease contracts throughout the country.

There are two underlying reasons why Sizzler found itself saddled with so many operating units with uneconomical leases. The first reason is that in Sizzler's two most developed markets, Southern California and the San Francisco Bay Area, the company simply built too many restaurants. From the outset of Jim Collins' acquisition of the Sizzler chain from Del Johnson, the revised Franchise Agreement developed by Sizzler's new owners provided a protected territory surrounding each unit within which no other Sizzler could be built. This protected territory was a radius of one and one-half miles around each Sizzler. To me, a one and half mile radius of protected territory never made sense. Given the amount of money it took for land, building, equipment and start-up costs to build a Sizzler, the notion that the population within a mile and half of a unit was sufficient to profitably support that investment was utter nonsense. This was true in the nineteen-sixties and early nineteen-seventies when the cost to open a Sizzler was a fraction of what the newer stores cost. Thus, by inference one can reasonably conclude that it made even less sense when Sizzler began building substantially more elaborate restaurants with a capital investment in land, building, equipment and startup costs approaching two million dollars and substantially remodeling their older units throughout the late seventies and nineteen-eighties.

Nevertheless, the one-and-a-half-mile radius of protected territory in the franchise agreement never changed significantly. (In the late nineteen-eighties it changed a little when the protected territory became a one-and-a-half-mile radius or an area encompassing 80,000 people, whichever was *less*). Of course, without regard to how much protected territory a franchised Sizzler was allocated, Sizzler corporate was free to set different guidelines for corporate store development. Be that as it may, the guideline to which it held itself accountable was the same--or less! Sizzler actually built a new unit in Colma, a community in the South San Francisco Bay Area which was only one-half mile away from one of its units in Daly City.

So, as the popularity of Sizzler increased throughout the nineteen-eighties combined with the ever-increasing economies of scale in television advertising as more Sizzlers were built, senior management turned a blind eye toward the level of financial risk it was incurring by packing ever more units into a fixed geographic region. Along with the financial risk Sizzler imposed on itself, it did the same thing to its franchisees via a program it called its Area Development Agreement.

The essential idea of the Area Development Agreement was to give franchisees with aspirations of becoming multi-unit Sizzler operators a first right of refusal for developable sites within a specified micro-region of a major market. The Area Development Agreement required that a franchisee build a given number of units over a specified period of time within the defined micro-region. The number of units which a franchisee was obliged to build was predicated more or less on the basis of developing new stores within one and a half miles apart. Should a franchisee choose not to pack his or her micro-region as tightly as the Area Development Agreement required for fear of cannibalizing the sales revenue of an existing unit, Sizzler International was free to build units of its own or allow another franchised operator to build a new unit within that previously protected territory. Although, to the best of my knowledge, Sizzler never exercised its ability to encroach on a franchised operator's micro-region established in an Area Development Agreement, the threat of doing so was perceived by the franchisees as very real. As one franchisee put it, regarding his misgivings about building a new unit too close to one of his existing stores, Sizzler International gave him one of two choices: either you cut your own throat or we'll cut it for you.

In every case of which I am aware, the franchisee, occasionally against his or her better judgment, opened new units in the defined territory at a pace sufficient to keep Sizzler International at bay. This further compounded the over building of units in California and put a proportionately greater financial risk on the shoulders of its franchisees. As things turned out, *every* multi-unit Sizzler franchisee in the San Francisco Bay Area eventually went out of business.

The financial risk of which I speak inherent in over developing a given geographic territory has to do with the contractual commitment Sizzler and its franchisees made by entering into long term commercial leases and/or assuming large fixed debt obligations for land, building and equipment Even though Sizzler had no fixed debt obligations, the commercial leases to which it was a party essentially carry the same degree of financial risk as fixed debt--or more. That being that should there be a decline in a store's sales, for any reason, the percentage of gross sales consumed in fixed costs increases and if the sales decline is more than a few percentage points, the store will begin to suffer operating losses. Well, as things turned out, this is exactly what happened. Of course, no one in Sizzler, not senior corporate management or the franchisees foresaw the decline in sales that would be brought on with the Buffet Court repositioning. However, the fact that the economy of every developed country in the world suffers perpetually from business cycles including periodic recessions should have been adequately anticipated in Sizzler's growth plans. A fact, in retrospect, Sizzler management seemed to ignore.

When the recession of approximately 1991--1993 rolled across the country, it really rolled over California. Much more so perhaps than the rest of the country and persisted longer. The contraction in consumer spending on dining out dropped precipitously in California during this recession and Sizzler, saddled as it was with too many stores servicing too few customers, was immediately flipped on its back by the fixed cost burden of its commercial lease obligations.

Moreover, the problems brought on by over building the California Market only tells half the story of the financial risk Sizzler incurred through its leased properties. The other part of this story has to do with the specifics of the commercial leases *per se*.

One of the legacies of the Carter Administration was the realization that inflation, previously never climbing higher than around six percent a year and usually remaining in the three to four percent per year range in this century could climb astronomically under the right--or should I say wrong--circumstances. A segment of the population especially hard hit by the runaway inflation of the late nineteen-seventies and early eighties were landlords whose properties were tied up in long term commercial leases with insufficient provision in their contracts to adjust the rent to adequately reflect the substantial decline in the purchasing power of the dollar or the increase in the fair market value of their real estate. Therefore, as old leases expired and in virtually every case where vacant land was developed, all new long term commercial leases provided for increases in the rent to keep pace with inflation. For the most part, the way this was accomplished and continues to be accomplished today is a requirement in the lease that the rent be adjusted upward periodically--usually annually--by an amount equal to the increase in the Consumer Price Index or some fraction thereof. In lease negotiation language this is referred to as a CPI COLA i.e., a Consumer Price Index Cost of Living Adjustment.

Undoubtedly, most of Sizzler's long term commercial leases obligated Sizzler to pay CPI COLA's sometimes with provisions for a minimum and a maximum adjustment. Whether or not any given lease provides the tenant some modicum of protection via a ceiling on the CPI COLA, no commercial lease of which I am aware, provides for a reduction in the rent under any circumstance. Thus, unlike a fixed debt obligation that remains constant over time, a fixed debt obligation assumed through a commercial lease always goes up.

This adjustment formula works fine and is fair for both the landlord and the tenant so long as the fair market value of real estate and the fair market value rent keep approximate pace with the Consumer Price Index. But this is not what occurred in the early nineteen-nineties. What happened instead was that as inflation, or more appropriately, the anticipation of an increase in inflation subsided, along with a contraction in consumer spending, the fair market value of commercial real estate dropped substantially across the country even though the CPI continued to go up at around four percent a year. Probably from the point of view of landlords, holding leases that mandated ever increasing rents, this was justifiable pay back for the losses incurred in the late nineteen-seventies thanks to Jimmy Carter. But fair for landlords or not, the economic reality is that sooner or later, there has to be a downward adjustment in the rent to adequately reflect the rent paying capability of the tenant. If not, the tenant will eventually go out of business and the landlord will be stuck with an empty building which can only be re-leased at a reduced price that would have allowed the previous tenant to remain in business in the first place.

The logic of a need for landlords to reduce rents to properly reflect the fair market value of their real estate has only been sporadically understood or appreciated. In some cases, landlords have refinanced their properties, taking out their increased equity from appreciated real estate values in cash, and assumed higher fixed debt obligations of their own predicated on the assumption of ever-increasing rent. In these situations, the landlords have put themselves in a damned if I do and damned if I don't predicament because if they lower the rent, they can't service their new, higher debt burden and if they don't lower the rent, the tenant will go out of business and they are in an even worse position. The options for a landlord who has refinanced a property in anticipation of steady or increasing rents only to have fair market value rents decline is one of a slow death or quick death--financially speaking. Given this option, the choice is always a slow death; i.e., don't lower the rent and hope to hell the tenant can somehow manage to continue to pay the tab.

Whether the landlords of Sizzler's operating units choose not to lower rents because of the slow versus quick death dilemma or whether it was simply a matter of believing they had their hand in a deep pocket and they didn't want to take it out, the effect on Sizzler was the same. Sizzler was committed to a sufficient number of excessively high fixed rent obligations that to do nothing meant the company would soon bleed to death.

For these reasons, Sizzler had to take some proactive initiative or face certain financial collapse. The course chosen was to declare Chapter 11 bankruptcy as a means by which to break its long-term lease contracts. If Sizzler's solution to its non-economic lease problem has not yet captured the attention every landlord and every institution that loans money secured with commercial real estate, it should. What may very well be a precedent setting action, Sizzler sought and was granted Chapter 11 Bankruptcy Protection at a time when its Total Assets were still substantially greater than its Total Liabilities. The company was granted protection from its creditors and afforded the opportunity to reject non-economic leases based on projections of what was going to happen in the future as opposed to a current insolvent situation. I think the CPI COLA rent increase provision that has become a mainstay of commercial leases, and perhaps even a perceived birth right among landlords is a contract provision that is overdue for extinction. The nineteen-nineties have proven beyond a shadow of a doubt that the Consumer Price Index and Fair Market Value rents can change in opposite directions simultaneously and some way to recognize this potential in long term leases needs to replace the conventional practice.

To a certain degree, Sizzler's financial problems were tied to non-economic leases resulting from assumptions made about the inherent compatibility of the Consumer Price Index Cost of Living Adjustments to rents and fair market value rents. It would be unfair to chastise Sizzler management too severely for this mistake. There is probably no other restaurant chain in the country that has not made similar commitments. In fact, I would be surprised to find more than a small percentage of the commercial leases negotiated by anyone in the last ten years that does not include some sort of rent escalation provision. On the other hand, the over development of the California market is a cross Sizzler management must bear.

Assuming most, if not all, of Sizzler's competitors have made similar lease commitments, then one might ask why many other restaurant chains are not doing the same thing. The main reason, I suspect, is that the effect of the recession, not compounded by other strategic marketing mistakes, was not severe enough by itself, to bring the company down. Had Sizzler's sales and customer counts declined in California by 5% or 10% or even 15% the company probably would have been okay by now. But Sizzler's unit sales and customer counts declined more like 40% to 60%. Clearly there were other factors besides the recession that cut Sizzler down.

Another blow to Sizzler was the loss of Jack Williams. Recall that I described Jack as the preeminent Sizzler franchisee. He was President of the National Sizzler Franchisee Association and was widely regarded both by the franchisees and senior Sizzler management as an entrepreneur's entrepreneur; Mr. Sizzler --the franchisee that all other franchisees respected and often tried to emulate. Jack Williams, the creator of the Sizzler Salad Bar was a true visionary restaurateur and most Sizzler franchisees stood solidly behind him in whatever posture he assumed regarding franchisor management practices, policies and procedures insofar as they affected the franchisees. Would Sizzler have pursued the Buffet Court so aggressively had Jack been around? Would the Sizzler Franchise Community have so passively accepted senior Sizzler management's decision to prematurely abandon the Buffet Court test and roll the program out system wide had Jack been around? These are questions to which there will never be an answer.

Jack Williams was lost to the Sizzler system in nineteen eighty-eight in a way that is really hard to imagine. For all of Jack's great strengths, unfortunately he had a weakness. Jack's partners in FORBCO caught him with his hand in the till in a very big way. As things turned out, it was discovered that Jack had embezzled several million dollars from FORBCO over a four- or five-year period. Upon this discovery, Jack was promptly fired as President of FORBCO and soon thereafter relieved of his post as President of the NSFA never to be heard from within the Sizzler community again. Although his partners did not press criminal charges, they required that Jack repay what he had stolen. After that, the IRS went after a piece of him and he was ultimately sentenced to serve a two-year term in Federal Prison for tax evasion.

Another weakness in the Sizzler system was the failure of the company to ever make any significant improvements in the Unit Performance Evaluation program originally developed by Walt Fitzgerald. As I expressed in the preceding chapter, the implementation of this program had a very positive affect on the systems overall level of concept execution and propensity to strive to achieve a high level of quality, cleanliness and service. Walt departed from this post in nineteen eighty-five and was replaced by Bob Zappelli. By and large, Bob's mission was to carry on the program first developed by Walt Fitzgerald and, in fairness to Bob, that's pretty much what he did, from nineteen eighty-five when he took over until nineteen ninety-two when he was reassigned to a different position in the company. The problem is that the full impetus of the Unit

Evaluation program to *improve* operation performance was achieved within a year or so of its introduction. After that, all the program ever achieved was the capability to more or less *maintain* the higher standard of performance it had brought about initially.

From the inception of the Unit Performance Evaluation program until it was discontinued in nineteen ninety-five, every Sizzler was inspected top to bottom every three months. Through this program Sizzler management was able to provide itself with an enormous body of performance data on each unit. But the resulting analysis of that data was pitiful. To the best of my knowledge, the only use to which the data was put beyond pointing out to each store manager where improvement was needed was to compute each Sizzler's score in terms of points earned as a percentage point possible and publish the results in descending score order. With these performance scores in hand, senior management used them in conjunction with various store manager performance bonuses and award programs that came and went over the years and for little else.

Sizzler management never learned how to effectively analyze the data. Had it done so, I believe that quite possibly the Buffet Court and certainly many of the numerous operational changes that senior management began imposing on the system as it struggled to overcome the problems brought on by the Buffet Court could have been avoided. One element of Sizzler Corporate Culture, especially in the early nineteen-nineties but generally throughout its history was an NIH mentality--Not Invented Here. Sizzler did not send its senior operations management to school nor did it hire individuals for these positions with advanced education nor did it appear to overly encourage creative thinking outside the marketing, product development and advertising function. Had it done so in short order I believe they would have fallen upon the concept of *Process Capability Analysis* which is one important element of a body of knowledge generally referred to as Statistical Process Control and/or Statistical Quality Control all of which in turn is embodied within the larger discipline now known in the United States as Total Quality Management.

The Unit Performance Evaluations consisted of around a hundred and fifty or so line items representing performance attributes subject to inspection. For years, the S.O.S. Department dutifully lined up each store's evaluation each quarter, added up the points earned by each store and computed that unit's score. It never occurred to Sizzler management to add the points earned by each store on each performance attribute *horizontally* and compute the average score to measure the *system's* performance or *Process capability* on any given performance attribute. Had Sizzler pursued this line of analysis and collated the results in descending average score order, it could have readily been able to identify various weaknesses in *system design* and therewith been able to appropriately address those problems *and* effectively differentiate between unacceptable unit performance on any given attribute and statistically acceptable performance given the inherent weaknesses and limitations of the system.

System Performance Summary	
	Possible
Kitchen	Points
Texas style ribs cooked to specs	100
Cajun style ribs cooked to specs	100
Order in to order out times within 12 minutes	200
Plate presentation meets specs	100
All equipment in good repair and operational	100
Total Points possible	600
Dining room	
Service staff following ten-step-service procedures	200
Guest check audits okay	100
Cash handling procedures being followed	150
Total Points possible	450
Food storage	
Refrigerator temps between 33-40 degrees	10
Freezer temps between 0-15 degrees	10
Storage locations properly labeled	75
Products in designated storage locactions	100
Stock rotation procedures properly followed	75
Total Points possible	270
Restrooms	
Clean	100
Checked every 30 minutes by staff	100
All supplies stocked	200
Facility in good repair and operational	100
Total Points possible	500
Administration	
Employee files current	50
I-9s completed properly	100
Cash management procedures being followed	200
Inventory forms completed properly	100
Cost control forms completed properly	100
Daily manager's log book procedures are followed	50
Total Points possible	600
Consolidated total points possible	2420

For example, consider the following charts which are intended to illustrate my point. The first chart does not represent the actual Performance Evaluation form Sizzler used. This chart illustrates the various line items representing performance attributes of *Billy Bob's Barbecue* restaurant, a hypothetical eatery I dreamed up for the purpose of this demonstration.

In this twenty-unit chain, the results recorded on the very bottom-line, Over-All Unit Performance are characteristic of the scores computed for each Sizzler. This score represents each store's ability to perform to specified standards. The audit form lists all the areas of the operation subject to inspection and the total points possible.

The points awarded by the inspector will be somewhat subjective however effort is made by management to provide the inspectors with reasonable rules-of-thumb.

In Sizzler's case, assigning points to each performance criteria and totaling them by department and by the consolidated total is all that was ever done with this data. Following, we will see what further analyses could have been developed with this data.

For the purpose of this demonstration, we will look at only the Food Storage section of the entire audit form. Each of the twenty stores are listed in the top row. Below are the points each unit received in each of the assessment categories. Also, assume that this report is the consolidated average of the past five quarters. The reason for an average of several quarters is to dilute the negative influence of a statistical outlier—i.e., a very low score received on one audit for some anomalous screwup unlikely to reoccur. To the right of the twenty stores' average points appear the twenty-store average, the standard deviation of the continuum, the control limit and the coefficient of variation.

The first of the following charts shows the points each unit received on each assessment category. Below that is the analysis of the data. The X represents the average points for a performance category not within the established acceptable range. For example, an X appears in store number one's *Storage locations properly labeled*. Two attributes are considered. The first is that only scores below the average value of 64.10 are considered. The other is that the score of 50 is below the Control Limit of 56.20 which is the lowest value within one standard deviation of the average.

Store Number	1	2	3	4	16	17	18	19	20
Refrigerator temps between 33-40 degrees				x		x			
Freezer temps between 0-15 degrees							x		
Storage locations properly labeled	x			x					
Products in designated storage locations					x			x	
Stock rotation procedures properly followed				x				x	

Store Number				1	2	3	4	16	17	18	19	20
Food Storage												
	Total Possible Points											
Refrigerator temps between 33-40 degrees			10	10	10	10	0	10	0	10	10	10
Freezer temps between 0-15 degrees			10	10	10	10	10	10	10	0	10	10
Storage locations properly labeled			75	50	69	73	53	73	58	60	68	67
Products in designated storage locations			100	99	91	99	86	77	82	98	76	94
Stock rotation procedures properly followed			75	56	64	68	52	62	71	67	50	50

Control Limit in Standard Deviations   1

Average Score	Standard Deviations	Control Limit	Coefficient of Variation
9.00			
9.50			
64.10	7.90	56.20	0.1263
88.10	9.11	78.99	0.105
60.85	6.72	54.13	0.104

Above is a summary of all twenty stores showing the average score for each category; the standard deviation, control limit, in this case one standard deviation, and the coefficient of variation.

There remains one remaining analytical step to consider and that is to list all twenty-five assessment criteria in descending score order. The lowest system-wide score would be at the top of the list. Given this chart format, management would immediately identify the relative strengths and weakness of the system design.

Now, let's consider the significance of the *coefficient of variation*. This metric is the standard deviation for one assessment category for all twenty stores divided by the array's average value.

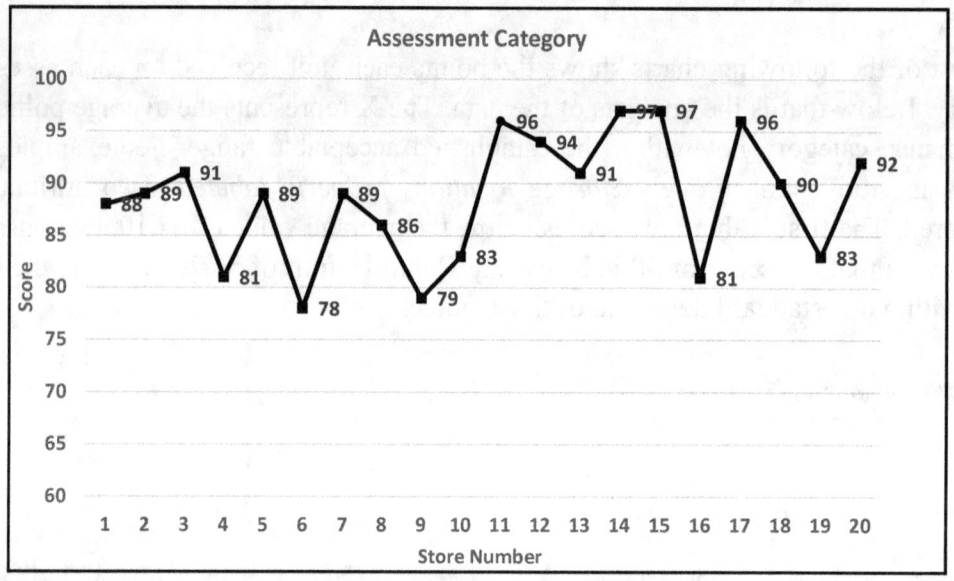

The object of this analysis is consideration for the *amplitude* of the oscillations. In a perfect world, all twenty stores would have the same score and a graphic depiction of this condition would result in a straight, level line. Of course, perfection is impossible. No matter what performance metric is under study, there will be inconsistencies across the continuum However, the underlying premise of this analysis is that all volatility is bad.

Thus, the issue comes down to what degree of volatility is acceptable. This is a matter of management judgement. In this example the coefficient of variation is .067 which, for the performance standard being measured, is low indicating that system-wide performance is under control.

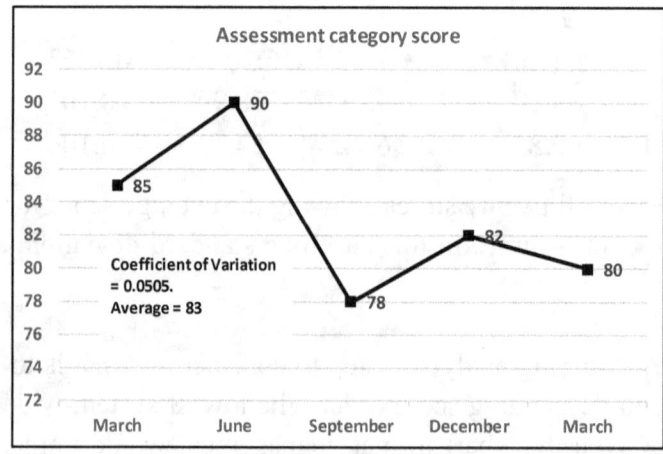

This volatility analysis could also be initiated on a store-by-store basis. In this case, the analysis continuum is time. The tacit assumption in this example that the range of the continuum must be at least five observations. Here again, the matter of acceptability for this degree of volatility is a matter of management judgement. Also, using time as the continuum, say on a monthly basis, the individual operating units' income statements could be subjected to the preceding analysis.

These analyses are all incapsulated within the practice of management known as *Management by Exception.* Management by exception is the practice of examining the financial and operational results of a business, and only bringing issues to the attention of management if results represent substantial differences from the budgeted or expected amount.[16] Management by exception imbues management with much greater focus than is possible without it. "Upper managers are well advised to *become knowledgeable about the growing role of the process capability concept,*" states Joseph Juran.[17] "It is now widely accepted that companies that make use of such quantification of process capability…will outperform companies that do not."[18] This is true because it has been fairly conclusively demonstrated that "between 85 and 98 percent of the problems in any firm are attributable to system design. The local employees are powerless to make lasting improvements."[19]

The mind set of senior Sizzler management was always that every failure of a unit to achieve an acceptable score on any given line item on the performance evaluation was an indication of unit level management weakness. There was never an adequate awareness of statistical quality control concepts and therewith the notion of Common Cause or Systemic problems which means individual failures to perform according to specifications due to flaws in the system design that prohibit acceptable performance and local fault or non-systemic problems which means individual failures to perform according to specifications attributable to that individual. The dual statistical quality control concepts of Common Cause and Local Fault problems and the requisite responsibility of senior management to assume *direct* responsibility for Common Cause problems and *directly initiate and participate* in efforts to develop system design solutions for them and only delegate solutions to Local Fault problems were ideas completely foreign to them. They essentially delegated the responsibility to correct all concept execution failures or improve the level of execution all the way down to the unit

---

[16] These analyses can be readily adapted to the analysis of a firm's variable costs on the income statement.

[17] Joseph Juran, *Juran On Leadership For Quality*, The Free Press, Copyright 1989; p. 127

[18] *Ibid.*, p.125

[19] Gary Fellers, *The Deming Vision: SPC/TQM For Administrators*, ASQC Quality Press, Copyright 1992, p. 136

manager in all situations. This resulted in an ongoing attempt over the years to solve all Common Cause problems with Local Fault solutions.

To be sure, the company developed operations improvement programs such as the P.R.I.D.E[20] program in the mid nineteen-eighties, followed a year or so later by M.O.R.E. P.R.I.D.E.[21] then followed by Sizzler's World Class program in the late eighties and ultimately Hugh Duncan's one such attempt called DAZZLE and finally, the last one of which I am aware, the BASICS program in 1994. But none of these programs included any sort of redesigning of the restaurant facility, the introduction of new operating equipment, menu modifications or other substantive changes to the way the work got done at the unit level that would enable the unit level employees to meet or exceed established performance standards with the same amount of effort, skills or knowledge. Essentially, these Operations Improvement programs were the establishment of upgraded performance expectations and standards delivered with the typical exhortations to try harder and do better along with the obligatory inclusion of various new rewards and punishments for meeting or failing to meet them. In the final analysis all that this really amounted to was yet another form of delegation wherein the mind set of senior management was that the responsibility to correct all operations deficiencies belonged to the unit level managers.

This is not to say that the unit level employees did not respond positively to these challenges because they did. The performance level of the system did improve somewhat from these efforts. However, there is a finite limit to how much improvement in system performance can be garnered through senior management edicts to try harder and do better, no matter what rewards and punishments are appended thereto. In the long run, all these programs typically accomplish is a temporary spurt in an individual's performance level or re-establish a previous unit performance level that was achieved in the past the last time senior management focused concentrated attention on it. The only time Sizzler was able to achieve and *maintain* a noticeable improvement in its level of operations was when it began publishing unit evaluation scores.

Beyond the launching of Operations Improvement Drives from time to time, the primary approach to improving operational excellence were the critiques which followed each quarterly Performance Audit and random visitations from various senior operations field commanders with such titles as District Managers, Market Managers, Operations Vice Presidents plus, in franchised outlets, Owners, etc. The quality of direction provided unit managers by these visitors though always well intentioned, was, to put it kindly, inconsistent. No doubt my view is somewhat biased, however, I believe the quality of training, coaching, guidance and just all-round general assistance provided unit level

---

[20] Provide a Really Incredible Dining Experience

[21] Make Our Restaurants Expert at Providing a Really Incredible Dining Experience

managers was, for the most part, superior in franchised operations than in corporate owned units. However, in all cases--both in franchised and corporate owned stores--there was never any program or system instituted by a corporate district manager or franchisee that resulted in a permanent, quantum improvement in store level operations. Had there been, it would have been evident in that DM's or franchisee's capability to produce consistently top-level Performance Audits quarter after quarter. This never happened.

Most of the time, the type of direction typically provided unit level managers was not much more than a spot check of conditions within a unit at the moment along with a review of the most recent store-level Profit & Loss statement and/or related interim performance data coupled with demands to improve performance deemed to be substandard, perhaps with some suggestions as to how to do that. This sort of direction has been defined by Tom Peters as Seagull Management. That is to say, the district manager flies into the restaurant, craps on everybody, then flies out.

It would be unfair to characterize all above-store-level operations managers in this way or to say that this was the only kind of direction unit managers received. Much attention was given by the company to the training and development of their unit level and district level operations management staff over the years. In fact, from around 1989 until around 1994 the company maintained a "management development" program based at the California Polytechnic University's Pomona campus known as Sizzler University. The program was open to any franchisee or franchisee's unit managers and attendance was more or less mandatory for corporate store unit managers. This was an excellent program and the unit managers I sent through the school all came away with a very positive attitude toward the experience. However, this program came late in Sizzler's history and was one of the first luxuries to be eliminated once the company started having cash flow problems. Additionally, there were always those special District Managers in the system who perceived themselves to be coaches or mentors for the unit managers in their charge and possessed the wherewithal to carry out their supervisory responsibilities in that spirit.

Nevertheless, Seagull Management was the principal method by which Sizzler unit managers received day-to-day direction and Performance Improvement Drives were the only method employed in efforts to raise the performance level of the system as a whole. Unfortunately, the long-term effect of Seagull Management on a system's performance is *not* benign. The typical justification that I have heard for this management tactic holds that even though such performance oversight may not do a lot to bring about a permanent long-term improvement in performance, it certainly can't be harmful and for a while at least, brings performance back up to snuff. However, as Statistical Quality Control theory predicts with a fair degree of mathematical certitude, most failures in performance execution are attributable to system design flaws, not employee shortcomings. More importantly, the inevitable long-term outcome of assuming performance problems is the result of employee deficiencies and therewith applying Seagull Management, to what are really system design problems will be *a decline in system performance*.

To say that senior Sizzler management had the operations staff and franchisees alike constantly chasing our tails with an unending cacophony of exhortations to try harder and do better replete with zero defect posters, Safety First posters we try harder buttons, award programs, plaques, Certificates of Achievement, unit inspections, Performance Improvement Drives and occasional threats would be an understatement. In retrospect, it's sad to think of all the effort, all the frustration and all the haranguing that went for naught among Sizzler's operations staff and franchisees when all the while Sizzler senior management had at its fingertips the system performance data necessary to identify operating system design problems and therewith the key ingredient necessary to develop design solutions via the application of Statistical Quality Control.

Another example of Sizzler senior managements' failure to adequately assess all the avenues available by which to achieve a competitive advantage was its failure to appreciate the potential inherent through the implementation of automated data processing at the unit level. In my company and in many other franchised Sizzlers throughout the country, Sizzler franchisees had jumped on the minicomputer bandwagon early on and implemented numerous innovative solutions to wide array of unit level administrative tasks and performance analyses. As a result, the time required to complete these tasks was reduced substantially and the accuracy with which they were completed was greatly improved. In addition, it became possible to provide the unit managers with detailed and near-real-time restaurant performance feedback that simply could not be done by hand.

For example, by feeding time card data into a macro driven Lotus 1-2-3 spreadsheet, my unit managers had a daily accounting of labor cost and labor productivity defined as customers served per labor hour broken out by departments for the day, week-to-date, week, month-to-date and month. It was routine in my company for each store manager to compare his or her unit's labor productivity of cooks, cashiers, dining room wait staff, salad bar attendants and utility staff—bus persons and dishwashers, as well as the average hourly wage within each department plus over all totals with the performance data from my other stores. Essentially, we were able to establish companywide labor productivity guidelines by department and generate daily feedback on performance to guidelines in great detail. The result was an ability to maintain tight unit level and companywide labor cost control

The formula by which to determine an operation's labor productivity is the average hourly wage divided by the average revenue per customer divided by labor cost's percentage of sales revenue. The methodology was invented by myself and my Vice

President of Operations Rick Page. Just for fun, we submitted it to a business journal and it was published.[22, 23]

I sent a copy of this journal article to Sizzler headquarters and management implemented it in their stores. However, the feedback on unit labor productivity in the corporate owned stores was limited to a break-out into two departments: Front of the House and Back of the House. Moreover, this information was only available to unit managers once the data was processed at their various regional headquarters following each payroll. There were efforts made here and there by unit managers to do some in-house analyses of labor data but it was mostly done by hand thus the accuracy and consistency with which it was done was sporadic. Some units had DOS versions of Lotus loaded into the 286 processor computers which Sizzler used to run their cash registers. However, these machines only carried about 1 megabyte of RAM and this put a severe limit on their capability to handle anything but the simplest of spreadsheets. Also, official corporate policy strictly prohibited unit managers from downloading copyrighted software due to a refusal to pay the necessary licensing fee. Thus, the limited automated analyses that were being done by unit managers was done so in secret using programs the managers brought from home. This fact essentially insured that no grass roots innovation would ever spring up and flourish within the company despite the burgeoning skill many managers were acquiring in the use of computers. As one might suspect, the fact that unit managers were required to spend a great deal of time recording data and producing various analysis of the data with only the help of a calculator when they knew full well this work could much more easily, quickly and accurately be accomplished on a computer was a source of great frustration for them.

In my company we also developed the capability for each store manager to compute the unit's food cost on a weekly basis. Computing the cost of goods sold necessitates taking a physical inventory and to expedite that task we developed a program that would print out the physical inventory product line item counting sheet in *storage location* order. Thus, a manager would start at storage location A-1, Storage Rack A, Shelf 1, count and record the number of each item on that shelf then proceed to storage location A-2 and so on. This substantially reduced the time it took to complete the physical count which is by far the most onerous aspect of determining cost of goods sold. Once all the physical count data was keyed into the computer it was automatically and instantaneously resorted into Food Cost Group Category order and compiled with Food Purchases Data thus yielding a Cost of Goods Sold analysis by Group Categories--Meat, Seafood, Salad Bar, Beverages,

---

[22] For more detail on this subject see The Relationship of Labor Productivity to the Cost of Labor and Profitability in the Restaurant Industry by Toby Tatum and Rick Page in *National Productivity Review*, Winter Edition 1987-1988.

[23] Calculating labor productivity by job title is done using the formula 1/consolidated productivity = 1/cook's productivity + 1/cashier's productivity + 1/wait staff productivity + 1/salad bar productivity + 1/utility staff productivity. This requires that the income statement reports labor cost by job title.

Beer and Wine, etc., as well as Total Food Cost. In this way, management in my company at all levels had weekly feedback on cost of goods sold.

In the case of corporate operated stores, feedback on cost of goods sold was provided once in each accounting period and that information was not available until well into the next accounting period.

This is not to imply that the units owned and operated by Sizzler International had no control of food and labor cost. To the best of my knowledge, they did control food cost reasonably well, however I believe unit managers could have reacted more quickly to food cost problems when they did occur and the entire company could have done a much better job at labor cost control. In fact, after I sold my last Sizzler, I was hired by Sizzler International as a consultant to help them improve their ability to control the cost of labor. One of the things I discovered was that labor cost as a percent of sales was nearly identical throughout all regions of the country. Considering the fact that around forty percent of corporate owned stores were in tip credit states, wherein the minimum wage for tipped employees was at the Federal Minimum of $2.01 an hour as opposed to $4.25 an hour in non-tip-credit states, it made sense that the labor cost percent should be lower in those states with the lower minimum wage. When I divided all corporate owned stores into two groups—tip credit and non-tip credit units—my analysis revealed that the group which enjoyed the lower minimum wage did indeed have a lower unit level average hourly wage but this was coupled with significantly lower labor productivity. The result of a lower average wage multiplied times the greater number of labor hours consumed to serve the same number of customers was that labor cost as a percent of sales was the same for both groups. I was able to demonstrate that if the company could achieve the same labor productivity in tip credit states that it was achieving in non-tip credit states, annual corporate profit would increase by almost two million dollars a year.

My final consulting assignment was to develop a computer program for use by unit level managers to better forecast customers and therewith improve their labor scheduling capabilities. I accomplished this assignment and then some. I included in this program what I considered to be a very sophisticated analysis of unit level management's ability to maintain control of labor cost and labor productivity via the application of a Shewhart Statistical Control Chart. This chart measured daily labor productivity performance variances and provided management with the capability to clearly identify if the store was operating within acceptable statistical control limits. It was my hope that through this innovation, I would therewith be able to introduce the company to a number of statistical quality control techniques I had learned to apply to a multi-unit restaurant environment

Unfortunately, no one but myself and Vicki, the manager of the Vallejo California Sizzler ever had the opportunity to see this system work. Before I could demonstrate the results of my work, the person to whom I reported, John Bayley, was laid off. I was then handed off to Bill Glasner, the head of Sizzler's Management Information Systems who quit two weeks later. I was then handed off to Tom McClune, John Bayley's assistant who subsequently quit three weeks after that. I was then handed off to Wayne McDaniels, Sizzler's Vice President of Operations. Within four weeks of this development and without any communication with me, Wayne had the computer and the program I developed for the company removed from the test store without my knowledge. No one from the company notified me that the test program had been terminated or that my services were no longer required. I simply presumed this to be the case since the computer and the program were gone. No longer having a computer or the program I developed in field test, I sent Sizzler a bill for my last visit to the test site, they sent me a check in the mail and that was the last contact I ever had with the company.

The foregoing is just some of the examples of the use to which PC's were put in one multi-unit franchised operation or could have been employed throughout the system. In my company we put those machines to many other uses as well, all with the aim to either reduce the time it required a store manager to perform necessary administrative tasks, improve reporting accuracy and/or improve the quality, quantity and turnaround time of various store performance analyses we felt essential to maintain constant control. Who's to say what would have been possible had Sizzler International put their time, money and effort behind a concentrated effort to harness the power of the computer at the unit level or at a minimum served as a collection and distribution point for the creative development work that was occurring within the franchise community across the country.

One perhaps can forgive senior Sizzler management to some degree for its failure to adapt to the computer age at the unit level or learn how to apply Statistical Quality Control concepts to its unit performance data. I doubt many restaurant chains threw their full weight into implementing sophisticated data processing at the unit level in the nineteen-eighties nor do I suspect there was one restaurant chain in a thousand, if indeed there were any, that were using state-of-the-art Statistical Quality Control concepts either because they didn't know how or because they were unwilling to incur the expense necessary to capture the requisite data. However, the concept of *consumer* research based on the statistical analysis of data gathered through customer opinion surveys is a well understood concept. There is no excuse for ignorance of this process yet Sizzler never in its history established a Market Research Department. This is not to say that the company never researched consumer opinions because it did but, for the most part, at least throughout the nineteen-eighties this research was conducted on behalf of Sizzler by BBDO and was focused primarily on consumer reaction to Sizzler advertising. BBDO did do some research on consumer opinions from time to time but it was an intermittent proposition at best. The kind of consumer research that Sizzler conducted internally can best described as collecting anecdotal responses to trial balloons regarding new products and promotional pricing strategy. Typically, a Sizzler Market Test consisted of putting a new product in a few stores close by Headquarters for a few weeks, aggressively promoting it, collecting sales data and asking the store manager what the customers told them they thought about it. The most telling value in this kind of consumer research is that, to the best of my knowledge, only one new product idea thus tested in fifteen years failed to achieve acceptable results and that was Turkey Marco Polo--really!

Although Sizzler management never learned much from this kind of research it was not a serious problem so long as they did not stray too far afield from the basic format. The problem though was that it never learned how to learn what consumers think and how they will react. Thus, when the Buffet Court was "test marketed" all Sizzler management knew how to do was what they had always done and in this case the conclusion reached was both wrong and disastrous.

Another disastrous failure on Sizzler's part, I think, was that the company did not properly size up the competition. To the best of my knowledge, efforts in this direction were largely anecdotal with the exception of the CREST survey which compared Sizzler system sales over time with the sales of other restaurant chains. There was never an ongoing statistically valid and reliable analysis of the perceptions and changes in perception among Sizzler's customers or the customers of its primary competitors until after it got itself in trouble with the Buffet Court. Thus, there was no adequate base line frame of reference against which to compare post-Buffet Court consumer impressions with pre-Buffet Court attitudes, or with the competition or, for that matter, to adequately analyze consumer impressions at the Buffet Court test stores during the test. A substantial amount of consumer research was initiated after Sizzler got into trouble but this was pretty much akin to closing the barn door after the cows were gone.

In one of my units in Sonoma County I began doing some limited competitive analysis using an analytical technique I developed myself. Within walking distance of one of my units there was an Olive Garden and a Red Lobster. Though somewhat clandestine means I was able to keep track of the sales in those two restaurants. The analytical approach I developed was to compare the *sales per square foot per month* of my store with those two competitors. What I discovered was that once the sales generating capability of each restaurant based on physical size was boiled out by computing sales per square foot, my Sizzler was performing *significantly* better than either the Olive Garden or the Red Lobster. From this I came to the conclusion that one should not limit an assessment of a unit's performance to a comparison of its current sales with its own sales in prior periods, either last month or the same month last year or make a straight across comparison of its sales with those of the competition.

In an expanding or contracting market, the only way to tell if a store is gaining or losing *market share* i.e., gaining or losing whatever consumer spending is available to get within the limits dictated by the physical capacity of a particular restaurant, is through competitive analysis. To only compare a unit's sales with itself in prior time periods in an expanding market, one could conclude incorrectly that if sales are going up one must be doing things right when, in fact, if the competition's sales are going up faster, one is doing things less well than its competition and is actually losing market share. On the other hand, if a unit's sales are declining in a contracting market but the competition's sales are contracting faster, then the conclusion should be steady as she goes because one is actually gaining market share. I raise this point because Sizzler's decision to develop the Buffet Court concept was largely a reaction to flattening system wide sales and customer counts. However, this was also the onset of a recession and it may very well have been that Sizzler was actually gaining market share relative to its main competitors in its various markets and therefore should not have made any significant changes to what it was doing.

Of course, it's far too late now to determine if this was indeed the case. However, had Sizzler adequately learned how to conduct effective competitive analysis along these lines, it is altogether possible that no serious thought or effort would have been focused on trying to invent new sales building programs but instead would have focused effort on how to improve the execution of its current concept.

In nineteen eighty the entire Sizzler system generated $259 million in annual sales. By nineteen ninety system wide annual sales had increased to just under a billion dollars. Undoubtedly, this kind of growth brings with it a need for ever greater sophistication in the management systems necessary to steer such a company. One of the fundamental management imperatives where Sizzler should have focused significant self-improvement efforts yet failed to do so was in their approach to Planning. To be sure, senior Sizzler management developed business plans. However, the *planning process* by which this was accomplished remained rather unsophisticated, in my view. The concept of *Strategic Planning* and the kind of planning process inherent in state-of-the-art Strategic Plan development never became a part of Sizzler's corporate culture. In fact, it was not until nineteen ninety-two that a business plan even referred to as a Strategic Plan was laid on the table. Sizzler senior management never subjected itself to a sufficiently thorough S.W.O.T. Analysis (Strengths, Weaknesses, Opportunities & Threats); never employed outside consultants to train itself in the art and science of leading edge Strategic Planning or facilitate the development of such a plan (with one modest exception that I will address later) and never asked itself what kind of organizational structure and what kind of individuals with what kind of experience are necessary to manage a billion dollar international company. Instead, Sizzler senior management attempted to break the billion-dollar barrier with a corporate culture not significantly different from that which existed ten years earlier when sales were only a fourth of their current level.

Although sales and profits continued to increase for Sizzler through nineteen ninety-two this was due to the incremental sales derived from new store openings. Any restaurant chain can increase total system sales at any time by opening new units. A better indication of how a restaurant chain (or any multi-unit retail operation) is doing is a comparison of same store sales from one year to the next. When examined under this light, one will find that annual increases in average unit sales and customer counts had started to flatten out by nineteen eighty-eight. In fact, the chain as a whole actually reached its peak performance in nineteen eighty-nine.

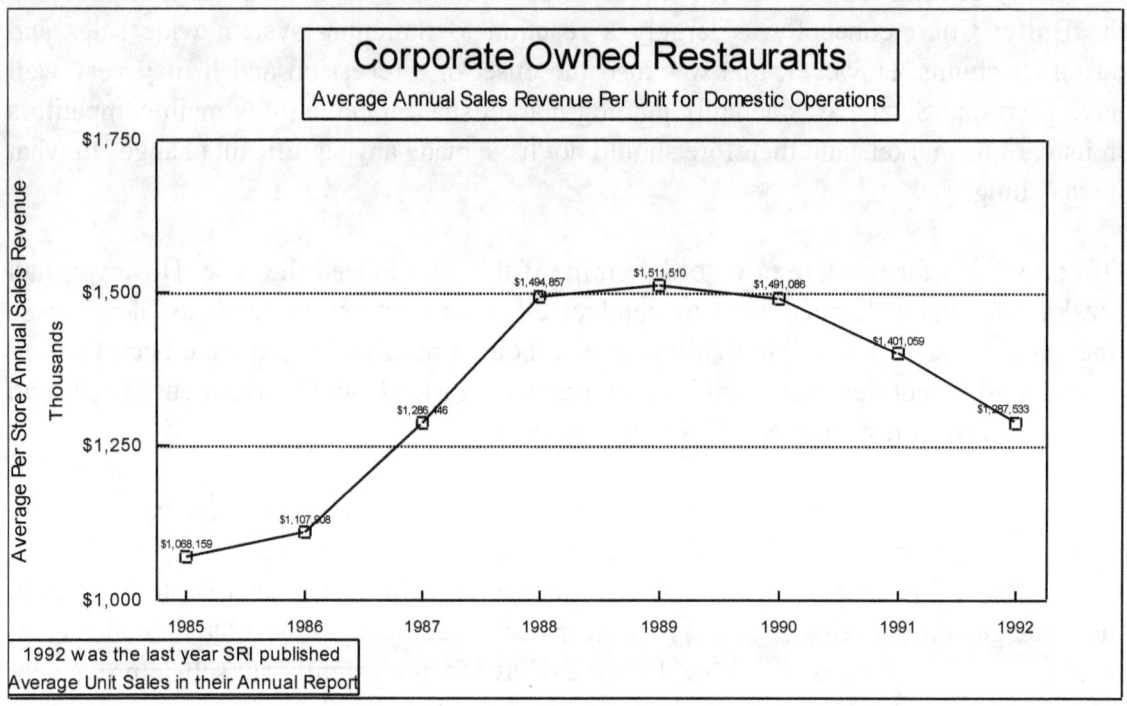

24

In theory of course, a restaurant must top out at some point because the physical limitations of a restaurant's four walls prevent it from increasing customer counts indefinitely. However, if this were the reason for the decline in the same-store sales growth rate, no doubt everyone with an investment in Sizzler would have been laughing all the way to the bank. But this was not the case. The production capacity of the units was not maximized. Moreover, if that *were* the case and there were no other underlying problems, then one would expect the trend line in the preceding chart to flatten out after reaching its peak, not decline.

What I believe was occurring was a decline the effectiveness of Sizzler's television advertising campaigns coupled with a blurring of Sizzler's image as a Budget Steak House brought about by the ever so gradual increase in the multiplier it used to determine

---

[24] The Per Store Average Sales depicted in the above chart were gleaned from the company's annual reports. 1990 was the last year this key performance statistic could be readily determined from the company's published performance data. After that, one has to read the fine print to get a sense of what was happening to PSA sales. From my personal experience, I know the decline which began in 1990 was never reversed at any period of time prior to the store closures concomitant with the declaration of bankruptcy. 1992 was the last year this performance statistic could be determined at all.

its retail markup over product cost. I believe this to be the case because by nineteen ninety or thereabouts, the system had pretty much come to rely on the Steak and All-You-Can-Eat Shrimp entree as its only effective television promotion. This is not to say that Sizzler promoted this product on TV to the exclusion of any other products, however the sales punch the other products garnered were becoming increasingly less effective. Moreover, the incremental sales generated by the Steak and All-You-Can-Eat Shrimp promotion was diminishing with each successive ad campaign as well.

The reason for this phenomenon no doubt was that the appeal of this product was dying out. Sizzler couldn't let go of the fact that when this product was first introduced on TV it generated the single biggest boost in sales of any new product introduction. As an interesting aside, I should point out that like the Sizzler Salad Bar, this product was also developed by a franchisee. In this case, it was Denny Robertson who, until the mid-nineteen-eighties, owned and operated about half the Sizzlers in the Chicago area.

However, Steak and All-You-Can-Eat Shrimp was a novelty or fad product and like any such product, has a short life then dies away. Once every one to whom this product had an initial appeal tried it a few times, I believe it eventually became evident to Sizzler customers that there was real value only for those who consumed an amount of shrimp in excess of the average consumption because that was the basis of its retail price. If a customer without a big appetite bought this product and didn't consume an amount of shrimp equal to the average, the product represented a low price to value relationship. In addition to this, I believe that even among our regular customers or loyal Steak and All-You-Can-Eat Shrimp devotees for whom this product represented a high price/value relationship, boredom was beginning to set in *and* that the constant barrage of Shrimp and other All-You-Can-Eat advertising campaigns were beginning to erode the public's perception of the overall quality of Sizzler's fare. More and more, Sizzler was acquiring a reputation as an all-you-can-eat restaurant even though the only all-you-can-eat product on the menu beside the Buffet Court was the all-you-can-eat shrimp entree with an occasional addition of all-you-can-eat beef bones for a few weeks at a time maybe once or twice a year.

By nineteen ninety, all Sizzler senior management and Sizzler franchisees were aware of the fact that Sizzler TV promotions were beginning to suffer diminishing returns and that our tried-and-true silver bullet—Steak and All-You-Can-Eat-Shrimp—was no longer working its magic. I am aware that this problem was the topic of serious discussion between Sizzler management and its account executives at BBDO. However, I have no knowledge of the substance of those discussions other than at times they were heated and that each was blaming the other for the problem. That is to say, Sizzler management was blaming BBDO for the declining effectiveness of its TV promotions, maintaining essentially that they had lost their creative edge while BBDO was saying that Sizzler's menu needed some revitalization—that there are just so many ways and so many times they could present one product before it finally wares out. In fact, probably both contentions were correct. In any case, the outcome of this line of discourse was that in March, 1992 Sizzler terminated BBDO as its advertising agency. Thus, ended what, for over twenty years, was perhaps one of the restaurant industry's most successful client/advertising agency relationships.

This action in turn necessitated Sizzler hiring a new ad agency. Keep in mind that Sizzler and BBDO joined forces by virtue of the fact that BBDO bought out Sizzler's former agency, Hall, Butler and Blatherwick. Thus, two decades had passed since the last time Sizzler senior management had to make an advertising agency hiring decision. The upshot of this fact is that among the ranks of current Sizzler management and the franchisees, there was very little hands-on experience in the process of advertising agency selection. Even if one gives Sizzler the benefit of the doubt that terminating BBDO was appropriate, I believe the company does not deserve such reservation for the manner in which it went about selecting its new agency.

Sizzler approached the agency selection process by selecting two candidate agencies and have them compete for Sizzler's account by staging demonstration advertising campaigns. Sort of an agency shoot out at high noon. To my way of thinking, this was nonsense. First, I believe Sizzler should have employed an outside consultant skilled in the agency selection process for companies of Sizzler's size and difficulties--especially considering the lack of experience for this process among Sizzler's current management. With the assistance of such a consultant, they probably should have assembled dossiers on agencies throughout the country with recent prior or even current mid-scale, casual dining restaurant chain experience or multi-unit retail chain experience, ideally with a reasonably long-term record for successfully increasing the average unit sales of its client(s) and then selected an agency with the best fit from that list.

But Sizzler would have none of this. They approached the project using the demonstration project approach and invited two Los Angeles based agencies to compete: Dailey and Associates and Chiat/Day. The outcome of these two dog-and-pony shows was that Dailey and Associates would be Sizzler's new advertising agency. Of course, the fact that one of Sizzler's newest members on its Board of Directors, Peter H. Dailey, was the founder of Dailey and Associates was explained away as purely coincidental. All were assured that Mr. Dailey had long since retired from his advertising agency, that no consideration of the fact that he founded this agency was made in the hiring decision, that he would not profit personally from the decision and therefore there was no conflict of interest.

As the saying goes, hind sight is always 20/20, and we can now see from the following chart that there were clearly some very serious problems brewing within the Sizzler system by nineteen ninety-two. Yet at that time, management's frame of reference was no doubt one of confidence in its ability to run a successful company. Had any one suggested then that the entire system was in the beginning stages of collapse its doubtful such a voice would have been able to garner much of an audience.

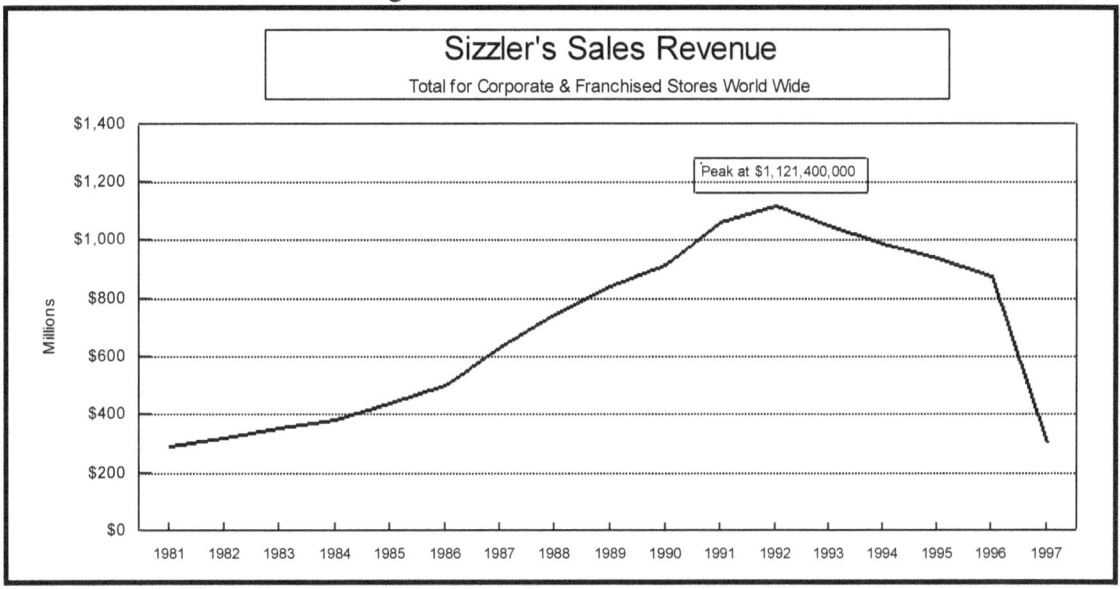

But the fact was that by nineteen ninety-two the Sizzler senior management team, management command and control systems, advertising agency and overall corporate culture, were not well positioned to run a billion-dollar international enterprise. From the many former Sizzler insiders with whom I have spoken during the course of writing this book, opinion is more or less split down the middle on whether Sizzler's eventual collapse was imminent by nineteen ninety-two or, alternatively, with a little luck and some capable leadership, the restaurant chain could have been able to overcome its internal weaknesses and molded itself into a genuine big-league player in time to avoid disaster. If the situation was salvageable, we'll never know. As we shall now see, probably the single biggest blow to Sizzler's competitive capabilities came in the form of an official change in senior management in early nineteen ninety-two which ultimately did the company in.

Chapter 5
Chaos and Collapse

In one important way, organizations are like trees: they die from the top down. In a publicly owned corporation, the Board of Directors represent the very top of the organizational pyramid and it was this body, led by Jim Collins that died first in my opinion--figuratively speaking of course. Certainly, by nineteen ninety-two but more than likely somewhere in the mid to late nineteen-eighties if not earlier, it appears to me Jim and the rest of the Board of Directors became completely complacent regarding both the strategic direction of Sizzler International and how day-to-day affairs were being managed. As the title of this book indicates, Sizzler International or more specifically, the stock holders, employees and franchisees of Sizzler International were the victims of gross negligence in my opinion. It's my guess that Sizzler's Board of Directors were, to some degree, lulled to sleep by their own PR such as the citation in the nineteen ninety-one Annual Report that a survey conducted by Forbs Magazine ranked the company as the 84th best performer in the nineteen-eighties out of 1,150 companies surveyed.

In my view, it was the Board of Directors in general and Jim Collins specifically who are most to blame for the collapse of Sizzler. The lack of a sense of a fiduciary responsibility to the company's stock holders despite the fact that Jim Collins' thirteen percent stake in the company was greater than any other single entity, and despite the fact that the State of Delaware's Corporation Code Section 141 requires that the business affairs of every Delaware Corporation shall be managed by its board of directors, is almost unfathomable (Sizzler's State of Incorporation is Delaware).[25] From all outward appearances, this body never acted as anything more than a figure head, and pretty much left senior Sizzler management alone to run the company as they saw fit probably with little critical assessment of management's performance and certainly without any remedial actions resulting from it. As we shall see, there would never come a time when the board felt compelled to step in, say enough is enough and therewith assume an active role in attempting to put the wheels back on the company even though I think the conclusion of any reasonable person has to be that that is what they should have done. In my admittedly layman's view, Sizzler's Board of Directors did not exercise an appropriate degree of Due Care.

It is important for one to keep in mind my assertion of the board's failure to exercise appropriate *Due Care* is a very significant criticism as the following suggests.

---

[25] Despite the decline in Jim Collins' person net worth of approximately seventy million dollars based on the spread between Sizzler stock at its highest of $20.75 a share and its current $2.50 a share, the impact on his lifestyle was minimal due to the fact that he reputedly received somewhere between 60 and 80 million dollars in Pepsi Cola stock in exchange for the KFC's he sold them. This was a tax-free exchange and this portion of his net worth was not reduced or put at risk by the decline of Sizzler International.

"For a director, exercising due care means acting on behalf of the company's stockholders by making informed decisions after obtaining all reasonably available information required to make an intelligent decision and after evaluating all relevant circumstances. Under this standard, the directors' duty is not merely to make the best possible decision for the corporation but to make their decision only after careful, informed deliberation. Both the process of decision making and the substantive decisions themselves are taken into consideration by courts in evaluating whether directors acted with due care. In the nineteen ninety-eighty-five Delaware case of *Smith v. Van Gorkom* the Delaware Supreme Court embarked down a road of increasing judicial scrutiny of business decisions. The court struck down the long-accepted practice of affording corporate directors the presumption that, in making business decisions, the directors acted on an informed basis, in good faith, and in the best interests of the company and shareholders. The court held that the determination of whether the business judgment of a board of directors is informed turns on whether the business judgment of a board of directors have informed themselves, prior to making business decisions, of all material information reasonably available to them. The court went on to say that, under the business judgment rule, there is no protection for directors who have made uninformed or unadvised judgments.[26]

Even if one is willing the forgive senior Sizzler management for not appropriately developing its strategic planning capabilities or operational control systems, it is hard to imagine its failure to concern itself with the issue of succession planning for the company's senior management. When Tom Gregory advised the Board in nineteen ninety eighty-nine that he planned to retire when he turned fifty-five in nineteen ninety-one one would think that Dick Birmingham, who, by this time was the company's Chief Executive Officer, together with Jim Collins and the rest of the Board of Directors would have turned immediate attention to hiring and cultivating Tom's replacement. In fact, they did absolutely nothing. When nineteen ninety-one rolled around, the Board of Directors, hat in hand, implored Tom to remain as President of Sizzler for another year. Tom agreed to do this but made it clear that on April 30, 1992 he was through. Given this reprieve, once again Dick Birmingham, Jim Collins and the board went to sleep and took no productive action nor developed any firm idea as to whom to hire as the new President.

However, approximately mid-way through Tom Gregory's last year, Dick Birmingham announced that he would succeed Tom as President of Sizzler. Dick Birmingham also indicated that Mike Minchin had been directed to begin cultivating his own replacement since Mr. Minchin was nearing retirement age. In response to this directive, late in nineteen ninety-one, a new number two man was brought into the Marketing Department,

---

[26] Stanley Foster Reed & Alexandra Reed Lajoux, *The Art of M & A: A Merger Acquisition Buyout Guide*, Copyright by The McGraw-Hill Companies, Inc., 1989 & 1995, pages 662 and 823.

ostensibly as Mike Minchin's protégé and heir apparent to the senior marketing position. His name was Hugh Duncan and the story fed to the NSFA Trustees was that Mike Minchin would cultivate Hugh Duncan over the next two years or so until his own retirement.

Although not a perfect transition plan, given the fact that Tom Gregory would be gone in six months, this sounded like the best plan possible. Dick Birmingham had been serving in a senior leadership position of Collins Foods International—Sizzler's parent company for over ten years. Therefore, this plan seemed to make some sense because the position of Chief Executive Officer as one separate and above the position of President of Sizzler no longer had any clear purpose. The company had long since shed itself of its wholesale food distribution company, Collins Food Service and had also shed itself of all Jim's Kentucky Fried Chicken outlets except for those in Australia, and had merged Collins Foods International into Sizzler International which meant that the company had only three divisions: Sizzler U.S.A., International Sizzlers forty corporate units and forty franchised units in Australia and 90 KFC's in Australia. Sizzler U.S.A. was far and away the company's largest division and the size and complexity of the other two divisions did not seem to warrant the need for a Chief Executive Officer to oversee three division Presidents. The notion that the positions of President of Sizzler U.S.A. and CEO of the entire company could be rolled into one position appeared completely logical.

Hugh Duncan's background, in turn, included a very successful career as an advertising executive where he eventually became President of the Foote, Cone and Belding/Los Angeles Advertising Agency. Mr. Duncan eventually left this position to pursue a career as a real estate developer which ended in bankruptcy and, no doubt, was the reason his services as a marketing executive were available for hire. Although Mr. Duncan's advertising experience did not include the management of a multi-unit restaurant chain account, it was still impressive and the general consensus was that with a few years of coaching from Mike Minchin, he would probably be able to hold his own as Sizzler's senior marketing executive quite well.

On the surface, the idea that Dick Birmingham should assume the consolidated positions of Sizzler International's President and Chief Executive Officer of Sizzler International also seem completely logical. However, a little critical thinking by any outside observer and a little deductive reasoning by the Board of Directors should have raised a red flag regarding Dick Birmingham's ability assume the day-to-day, hands-on management of the company.

The fact of the matter is that one of Dick Birmingham's principal occupations throughout the nineteen-eighties successively as Chief Executive Officer of Collins Food Service, Collins Foods International and Sizzler International was to oversee the development of new corporate growth vehicles. In that capacity, CFI with Dick Birmingham at the helm made an attempt to develop no less than nine different restaurant concepts. Either by way of hatching a brand-new concept, by acquiring a concept started by others or by acquiring territories in which to develop already established concepts, Dick had indirect but ultimate oversight of the corporation's efforts to develop H. Salt Esquire, the Taco Den (Australia), Gulliver's Cafe (Australia), Tony and Luigis, and Emmas Tacos. Dick assumed direct "hands-on" responsibility for the development of Ed Debevicks, Geno's East, Josaphinas and Buffalo Ranch. Every one of these projects were eventually abandoned.[27]

Somewhere along the line, the Board of Directors should have considered the odds against a truly capable executive having this long a string of bad luck. The amount of money lost in these projects ran into millions of dollars. Considering this track record, in retrospect it's hard to believe that Jim Collins and the Board of Directors would give Dick the responsibility to manage the goose that was laying the golden egg--but they did.

Although Tom Gregory did not retire until April 30, 1992, Dick Birmingham began to assume an increasingly more active role in the day-to-day affairs of Sizzler operations sometime late in nineteen ninety-one. With each passing month Dick began to usurp both Tom Gregory's and Mike Minchin's areas of responsibility and imposing his own ideas and edicts. In fact, Dick Birmingham inserted himself as Sizzler's new President prior to Tom Gregory's retirement. During the last several months of his Sizzler career, Tom Gregory was relegated to a back row seat, with responsibilities and task assignments that were obscure.

This is a gray area in Sizzler's history and in all probability only those three individuals have a clear idea of who was in charge of what during Tom Gregory's last year or so with the company. But if ever there was a time in Sizzler's history where capable leadership was needed, this was it. By early nineteen ninety-one it was quite evident that the Buffet Court, now installed in all U.S. Sizzlers, was a mistake and that some serious damage control was sorely needed. Yet, the decision, either by conscious design or due to disorganized leadership, was to forge ahead with the Buffet Court nevertheless.

So, it was on this sour note that Tom Gregory's career as the leader of Sizzler Restaurants International came to an end. By early nineteen ninety-two one could cut the feeling of foreboding that hung in the air over Tom Gregory's approaching departure with a knife. But Dick Birmingham attacked the situation with an ax. He used it to make his first significant command decision as Sizzler's new President. He fired Mike Minchin. Thus, Sizzler International now faced the future, beset with a clear and growing crisis, without the guidance of the two senior executives or the advertising agency that had led the

---

[27] There is one more new concept Sizzler took on. In 1995 Sizzler signed a deal to become a franchisee of the Italian Oven concept and develop 125 Italian Ovens in Australia. After Sizzler opened its first and only unit, the franchisor went bankrupt leaving Sizzler as an independent operator of one Italian restaurant in Australia.

organization from a relatively small regional company into a billion-dollar enterprise over the last ten years.

Without regard to whether or not Mike Minchin had lost his edge as Vice President of Marketing, the timing of the decision to remove him couldn't have been worse. Giving Dick Birmingham the benefit of the doubt that it was in the company's best interest to remove Mike Minchin, from a morale standpoint and from the need to further acclimate Hugh Duncan to the food service business, I believe that action should have been delayed by at least a year or that Mike should have been replaced by someone with multi-unit food service experience.

Be that as it may, with Mike Minchin's departure, Hugh Duncan became Vice President of Marketing. Instead of two or more years of coaching, he assumed this role with only a few months experience in the food service business. Presumably, in an effort to further improve Sizzler's Marketing Department Hugh Duncan and Dick Birmingham over the next few weeks terminated everyone in the small marketing staff that had reported to Mike Minchin. During this process, Sizzler hired Dave Barrows as the new number two man in the Marketing Department. They also hired Karen Garrell as the company's new Director of Product Development—later to be promoted to Vice President of Product Development. Karen Garrell was hired away from Stuart Anderson's Black Angus restaurant chain where she was employed in the same capacity. In an unusual twist of fate, the individual whom Ms. Garrell replaced, Stacey James, was then hired by Stuart Anderson's Black Angus as Ms. Garrell's replacement

Dave Barrows can best be described as an exceptionally intelligent, personable and talented individual with substantial food service field marketing management experience. As Sizzler's number two man in the Marketing Department, his only weakness was that his experience was limited to directing the execution of Taco Bell advertising and promotions—which was not really ideal given Sizzler's needs. Moreover, he had no leadership experience in developing system wide strategic marketing plans or working with a budget much smaller than that available to Taco Bell. His experience, in the capacity of a Regional Marketing Manager, was to implement the strategic plans developed by senior Taco Bell marketing management.

For better or for worse, Sizzler's marketing team now consisted of a Marketing Vice President with no restaurant experience whatsoever and an assistant director with only Taco Bell field level marketing experience.

To say that Dick Birmingham was undaunted by this clear weakness in the senior management team he was building would be an understatement. In February, 1992, approximately six months into his reign as Sizzler's new President, Dick decided to abandon that role and once again serve only as Sizzler's Chief Executive Officer. He appointed Hugh Duncan President of Sizzler U.S.A. and Dave Barrows was promoted to Vice President of Marketing.

To make matters worse, by this time, Sizzler no longer had a Vice President of Operations. That position had been eliminated and replaced instead with four Regional Operations Vice Presidents who all reported to the President. Whether Hugh Duncan actively sought the position of President or it was foisted upon him, given Sizzler's growing Buffet Court crisis, the lack of depth in the Marketing Department and lack of anyone in charge of Operations, in my view it was not reasonable for him to think he could effectively manage a restaurant company with over ten thousand employees spread out to all four corners of the country considering he had no prior food service management experience.

This reorganization of Sizzler's senior management was met with surprisingly little complaint. Whether it can best be attributed to mass denial or some other psychological defense mechanism, I was amazed by the lack of protest. The very minute I learned of Hugh Duncan's promotion to Sizzler's President I called Ron Higgins, the current President of the National Sizzler Franchise Association. I told him I was dumbfounded by this move and further asserted in no uncertain terms that, in my opinion, this was an alarming sign of incompetence on Dick Birmingham's part. Over the course of the next few months, I took it upon myself to express my concerns to the other twelve members of the Board of Trustees of the National Sizzler Franchisee Association. Some seemed to grant my concerns a modest degree of plausibility but most, as best I recall, seemed to accuse me in one way or another of behaving like Chicken Little. In fact, there were other NSFA Trustees who though Hugh Duncan's promotion was a good move. *Nation's Restaurant News* interviewed O'Neill Printy, a 10 Unit operator in Santa Clara, California where he is quoted as saying he believed Hugh Duncan to be very qualified for the job. In the same article Christopher Thomas states that "Hugh Duncan may not have run restaurants specifically, but he has run businesses."[28] Mr. Thomas neglected, of course, to mention that Mr. Duncan's last business venture ended in bankruptcy.

Starting with the ascension of Hugh Duncan to President of the company in February, 1992 I don't think I ever got a good night's sleep for the remainder of my time with Sizzler. Sizzler per store average sales and customer counts continued to decline and all the while, the decisions, actions and pronouncements forthcoming from SRI Headquarters continued to make less and less sense.

For those whose only idea of what was happening inside Sizzler came from what they read in the company's Annual Report, it is likely their perception of what lie ahead for Sizzler Restaurants International was entirely different. Although per store average sales and customer counts were on the decline within the U.S., system wide sales revenue

---

[28] *Nation's Restaurant News*, February 24, 1992

including revenue from foreign operations were at an all-time high. Sizzler's Annual Report dated April 30, 1992 reported record system wide sales of $1,121,400,000. This was due to the fact that both SRI and franchisees were still opening new units in addition to the development of new foreign operations. Everyone's assumption at this time was that the Buffet Court Problem would ultimately be resolved and things would get back on track soon enough. There were now 721 Sizzlers in operation including 83 on foreign soil. Because of the problems Sizzler was having in the U.S., plans to grow the system were predicated primarily on growing the international division. In Sizzler's previous Annual Report for the fiscal year ending on April 30, 1991 the company estimated that more than one hundred Sizzlers would be operating outside the U.S. within three years.

However, within eight months of Sizzler's record annual sales revenue performance, that is, in January 1993, the cash flow in my company turned negative and I began consuming my cash reserves which at that time were around $100,000—about enough to remain in business approximately six more months in the absence of some serious cost reductions. This occurred despite many cost reductions actions I initiated throughout nineteen ninety-two including reducing my own salary from $250,000 a year to $150,000 a year. In March, 1993 in an effort to re-acquire a positive cash flow, I reduced my salary once again from $150,000 a year to $60,000 a year and around April of 1994 I had to reduce my salary to zero where it remained until I ended my Sizzler career seven months later. Unfortunately, this measure was not sufficient to stop the bleeding. There was only one way left that I could see to further cut costs and that was to discontinue paying my "voluntary" additional contribution over and above my contractually required contribution to the Bay Area Cooperative Advertising Fund. My Sizzler Franchise required that I contribute three percent of gross sales to this fund, however in the mid nineteen-eighties all the franchisees in the greater San Francisco Bay Area and Sizzler corporate agreed to pay an additional one and a half percent of sales into the fund with the clear understanding that this payment was voluntary and any franchisee or Sizzler corporate could renege on this commitment at any time. So, in March, 1993, I decided to reduce my company's contribution to the advertising fund by discontinuing to pay my voluntary contribution of one and a half percent of sales. This amounted to a reduction in my contribution of approximately $6,000 a month. I notified Sizzler of this decision in writing and further pointed out that I had also reduced my own salary by $7,500 a month and also reduced the salary of my Vice President of Operations by $2,000 a month. I explained that I had to take this action immediately otherwise I would soon be out of business and with that the Bay Area Advertising Co-op would lose my ongoing contribution of just under $14,000 a month.

The initial word I got back from Sizzler headquarters was that I couldn't do what I had just done; that my "voluntary" contribution had ceased to be voluntary at some point in time and that I must continue to pay the additional $6,000 a month. This difference of opinion was quickly resolved in my favor and Sizzler corporate reluctantly had to accept my decision. However, things didn't end there. Within a couple of days of being notified that I was not in violation of my franchise agreement, I received a call from Dick Birmingham. This was the only time he ever called me. He expressed his dismay at my decision and said that by doing what I had done, I had set a bad precedent which was unacceptable apparently ignoring or oblivious to the fact that I was *not* the first franchisee in the Bay Area to renege on the voluntary contribution. The first to drop out was Barry Rahn who owned three Sizzlers in Silicon Valley. He indicated that he felt it necessary to make an example of my decision with an appropriate corporate response. The official corporate response to come out of all this was that Sizzler would reduce the advertising contribution of all of its stores in the Bay Area by the same one and half percent. This meant that the Bay Area Advertising Fund contribution would be reduced by approximately $60,000 a month plus my reduction of $6,000 a month.

The $60,000 a month reduction in the Bay Area Advertising Fund was a devastating blow. It effectively ended Sizzler's ability to maintain a continuous presence on television in that market. Considering the fact that a continuous television presence was Sizzler's principal competitive advantage, I still find it difficult to believe that the President of a public company would so severely undermine the competitive strength of its second largest market apparently just to get even with a six-store franchisee.

In all regions of the country, Sizzler's sales and customer counts continued to decline and time became Sizzler's principal enemy. There was never enough time to fully develop a workable resolution to the growing crisis. The strategy adopted became an unending and desperate quest for a silver bullet. Thus, new products began to roll out of Sizzler's test kitchen seemingly on a daily basis. The aim was either to come up with something so unique that everyone would have to come to Sizzler to try it or to come up with something we could sell so inexpensively that the public could not afford *not* to return to Sizzler for such a bargain. Unfortunately, this approach to rebuild Sizzler did not work. In ever increasing numbers, the public demonstrated their disapproval of this strategy by voting with their feet and visiting the competition.

The NSFA Board of Trustees became increasingly vocal about the need to stabilize the system and suggestions that Sizzler develop a Strategic Plan became more and more frequent. In response to these suggestions, Hugh Duncan took it upon himself to develop such a plan. Whether Mr. Duncan lacked knowledge of how a Strategic Plan should be developed or whether he felt there was insufficient time to subject the company to the rigors of a thorough strategic planning process, the resulting product was nothing more than an eighteen-page to-do list he developed by himself over a three- or four-week time period. Copies were given to all the Trustees with some modest fanfare at a meeting in Los Angeles and that was pretty much the end of it. The document had no legs and was soon forgotten.

The announced new strategy for Sizzler was to become a family restaurant. That this was pretty much what we already considered ourselves to be seemed beside the point.

Actually, what seemed to be occurring was a phenomenon best described as putting the cart before the horse. Top management would come up with some new product idea and having that in the bag so to speak, would invent a new Corporate Vision that fit the new product. By this time, strategic talk had become fashionable in the organization even though any knowledge of bona fide strategic planning was as foreign to the company as ever.

The central element to our new family restaurant repositioning was the Kids Bar. Yet another satellite bar was being added to the array of bars in the dining room which in many cases necessitated the removal of even more tables and chairs. The Kids' Bar was designed to look like a street vendor push cart, complete with umbrella offering assorted foods having specific appeal to small children. In addition to this new bar, we were required to incorporate a new store level staff position called The Kids' Host. The function of this individual was to assist kids at the Kids Bar and generally just walk around the dining room and entertain little kids.

The fact that what was most needed was a strategy to get us out of the Buffet Court program seemed not to phase senior management at all. Dick Birmingham, who had evolved into sort of a shadow President or co-President with Hugh Duncan was so convinced that the Kids' Bar and Kids' Host would turn Sizzler around that he had Kids Bars built as fast as possible, installed in all corporate stores and sent free of charge to all Sizzler franchised stores. With great fanfare--Sizzler was really getting good at announcing new turn around strategies--the Kid's Bar program was rolled out across the country and TV commercials depicting it were developed for airing in every market. Within about six months after the roll out of this program it was declared an unequivocal success by virtue of the fact that system wide sales had only declined by another three percent as opposed to the approximately six percent decline suffered in the previous six months although labor cost had risen slightly due to the addition of the Kids' Host. Sizzler was getting good at self-delusion also. So much so that it was featured prominently in Sizzler's nineteen ninety-three Annual Report as a central feature of the company's plans to revitalize sales.

But the new products continued to be rolled out. So many in fact that it's impossible to recall them all. However, there are a couple that deserve honorable mention: Australian Baked Chicken and Sea Monsters.

Despite the fact that every attempt to launch a new product as Sizzler's silver bullet failed to halt the downward trend, hope sprang eternal. One of the new products upon which Sizzler really placed high hopes was Australian Baked Chicken. As new products go, this one was not bad. In fact, it was really pretty good, and it could be retailed for around five dollars and yield an acceptable profit. The idea behind the merchandising was to romance the customer with a novel product with an Australian appeal to play off the country's fascination with things Australian, no doubt attributable in part to the popularity of the

Crocodile Dundee movies. However, truth be known, the product was really a recipe copied from a popular Cuban restaurant in Culver City, California called *Versailles*. Moreover, despite the additional intended appeal of being a baked product, and therefore better for you, the fact was that this product was prepared by first baking the chicken about half way done, refrigerating them and then preparing them to order by deep fat frying them for an additional five to seven minutes.

Whether or not most customers caught on the fact that their baked chicken was really baked, then fired chicken or, if they did, whether or not they cared is academic at this point. The product, although gaining a permanent place on Sizzler's menu for a couple of years or so, did nothing to turn around the sales and customer count decline.

Sea Monsters were a fiasco. This was one of Dick Birmingham's pet projects and his idea was to offer something that no other restaurant could copy. Sizzler got a line on a species of craw fish grown as farm animals in Mainland China and nowhere else. So, to ensure that no other company could copy this new product assuming anyone would want to, the company bought China's entire harvest for one year. The finished product was a shelled, de-veined craw fish which was breaded and deep fat fried. It was merchandised using in-store posters and hanging banners plastered with pictures of sea monsters which were nothing more than little happy faces. Never mind the fact that these were fresh water animals. The corporate decision was to merchandise them as Sizzler's latest addition to its seafood menu selection. The program was a dismal failure and Sizzler was stuck with tens of thousands of pounds of Chinese Craw Fish that it couldn't sell. As far as I know, those things are still in some freezer collecting ice crystals.

One of the means by which Hugh Duncan and Dick Birmingham attempted to find solutions to Sizzler's problems was the creation of a Concept Committee comprised of Hugh Duncan, Dick Birmingham, Jim Collins and four members of the Board of Trustees of the National Sizzler Franchisee Association. I was one of the individuals appointed to this committee. Our mission was to explore and discuss ideas, opportunities and alternative solutions to Sizzler's current challenges in an effort to re-establish the company as a viable restaurant concept.

The Concept Committee was organized about the same time that the Kids' Bar was under discussion as one possible solution. The fact of the matter was that the decision to launch the Kids' Bar program had already been made and the Concept Committee's first meetings were focused primarily on an appropriate pricing strategy. The President of Dailey & Associates attended one of these meetings and made as forceful an argument as possible to offer it free of charge to children under a given age. I think he said "under ten." This recommendation didn't get very far, but I learned an important lesson from this meeting. That is, that it is imperative that a company keep its advertising agency on a short leash. In my opinion, what the advertising agency was looking for was a way to escape the necessity of having to be creative. Clearly, the easiest way for an advertising agency to generate incremental traffic for a client is the announcement that the client is giving their product away free. To be sure, if the Kids Bar or any product Sizzler offered were given away free, an increase in customer counts would likely result. However, the object of the game is to make a profit and give-away programs are not the way to do that. Ultimately, we decided to charge $1.99 for the Kids' Bar but after its system wide roll out, a whole range of different pricing strategies were used in an attempt to generate incremental traffic.

Early on in my role as a member of the Concept Committee, I became frustrated with its lack of any clear direction. There was no real substance to our meetings beyond brain storming new product ideas, hearing about the progress of new product development projects from Karen Garrell or discussing what price we should charge for those products. We were flailing at the wind. We were not discussing concepts at all. To me it seemed this committee was nothing but another attempt to find the silver bullet that would save the day for Sizzler. In part as a result of my frustration with the meandering direction of the Concept Committee and in part out of a genuine desire to offer something of substance to the group, I requested and was granted the opportunity to make a special presentation.

Perhaps a year earlier, I had become a student of the concept of Total Quality Management. I had read a large number of books on the subject, had introduced the idea of TQM to my management staff and had implemented some TQM initiatives in my own company. With this knowledge and experience, I felt comfortable and qualified to present the concept of Total Quality Management to senior Sizzler management and felt the Concept Committee was the ideal place to take this step. I knew I had to take my best shot because I would only get one and the approach I used was a video presentation of an introduction to Total Quality Management produced by the Juran Institute.[29] This was a superbly produced half hour introduction to TQM replete with multiple testimonials from the CEO's of various companies across the country describing the significant improvement in product quality, cost control and bottom line results they had achieved by becoming a Total Quality Management company.

My hope was that this video would prove inspirational to the committee and that Hugh Duncan, Dick Birmingham and Jim Collins would see TQM as a possible organizational platform upon which to strive to rebuild the company. I truly felt that I was providing the company at last with their elusive silver bullet. To say my expectation was naive would be an understatement. The feedback I received following this presentation was complete, total, utter silence. The committee immediately thereafter adjourned for lunch and I never heard a word about this presentation from anyone at any time that day or thereafter. It

---

[29] The Juran Institute is a private training center established for the benefit of practicing managers by Dr. Joseph Juran. Dr. Juran is one of the world's leading authorities on the training and practical application of Quality Improvement skills.

became clear to me that the last thing Sizzler's Concept Committee wanted consider were concepts.[30]

However, I remained steadfast in my efforts to try to affect change in Sizzler's direction through my position on the Concept Committee. In fact, I used this committee as the venue in which to express my concerns with the performance of our advertising agency which was another source of my frustration with the direction Sizzler was headed.

It may be unfair to be overly critical of Dailey and Associates performance because their mission was increasingly becoming one of trying to make a silk purse out of a sow's ear. However, one thing I learned from many years of listening to post-promotion analysis presentations submitted by our advertising agency whether it be BBDO or Dailey and Associates is that no matter how well or poorly a particular promotion went, the performance data developed by the agency will clearly show that the agency is doing a good job *and* that if we invest just a little more money in advertising, we will break through a new threshold where the return on our incremental investment will be substantial. Over the years by this time, I had probably looked at a thousand different charts, graphs and other presentations, all very professionally done, frequently multi-colored developed specifically for this purpose. When it comes to schmoozing clients, advertising agencies rank among the best there is. By this time, however, my patients with this self-serving banter had finally come to an end. Rather than just accept what the agency chooses to spoon feed us and walk away happy, I took it upon myself to critically analyze the performance data from one of their presentations.

I did not make many friends at the agency by doing this, but I felt it was time somebody said something. In December, 1992 I sent a letter to all members of Sizzler's Concept Committee wherein I submitted my analysis of Dailey and Associates' latest analysis of their performance in the San Francisco Bay Area. Among the stack of charts and graphs presented at that meeting were two that I used to take the agency to task. The first was a review of Sizzler's Share of Voice, i.e., Sizzler's percent of total advertising messages among those other restaurants advertising on TV the agency felt represented our primary competitors. Here's the first chart the agency presented which is the Sizzler needs to invest more money in advertising pitch:

---

[30] In 1995 under the direction of Kevin Perkins, Dick Birmingham's successor, the company would embark on a "reengineering exercise" predicated on the book Reengineering the Corporation by Michael Hammer and James Champy. My reading of that book led me to conclude that what they were espousing was fundamentally the same as what I had read in various books on Total Quality Management--especially the ideas of Joseph Juran. Indeed, some of the examples of companies that had successfully "reengineered" themselves cited in Messieurs Hammer and Champy's book were the same ones cited in the TQM literature as companies that had successfully implemented TQM.

Sizzler's share of voice has declined almost 30%, while Denny's, Black Angus and Chevy's Share of Voice has increased.

Bay Area Share of Voice

Restaurant	Advertising Expenditures 9/90--8/91	Share	Advertising Expenditures 9/91--8/92	Share
Sizzler	$3,700,000	40%	$2,700,000	34%
Denny's	$800,000	10%	$1,100,000	14%
Red Lobster	$1,500,000	19%	$1,200,000	15%
Chevy's	$400,000	5%	$600,000	8%
Black Angus	$700,000	9%	$1,300,000	17%
Marie Calendar	$500,000	6%	$300,000	4%
Totals	$8,200,000	100%	$7,800,000	100%

The second chart was used to show how well the television viewing public could remember Sizzler's and other chains' TV commercials. Here's the second chart the agency presented which is the we're doing a pretty good job pitch:

Although Unaided Awareness for Sizzler has been fairly flat, Total Awareness is higher this year versus last. Increases were also measured for five other brands.[31]

Total Awareness of Selected Restaurants Advertising
Unaided + Aided

	9/90--8/91	9/91--8/92
Sizzler	65%	75%
Denny's	57%	67%
Black Angus	31%	41%
Red Lobster	31%	57%
Chevy's	31%	51%
Marie Calendar	11%	21%

---

[31] Unaided Awareness is a measurement of consumers' ability to recall the substance of an advertising message without being prompted by the interviewer with specific brand names. Total Awareness is the sum of the Unaided and Aided Awareness score.

The foregoing two charts were all the data the agency presented on this topic and, as expected, were intended to (1) encourage us to spend more money on advertising and (2) pat themselves on the back.

In my letter to the Concept Committee, I added a third chart of my own. I called this my Bang for the Buck Chart. I theorized that if all the foregoing restaurant chains' advertising agencies were doing an equally good job, then the ratio of the Share of Voice, that is to say the ratio of the money spent on advertising by any one chain relative to the total should yield an equally predictable level of Awareness for the chain's current promotion among the consuming public. Conversely, if the different agencies were *not* doing an equally good job, differing levels of Awareness would result from any given dollar expenditure on advertising. In Sizzler's case, for September, 1990 through August, 1991, the level of Awareness its advertising produced was 65% while the money Sizzler spent on advertising represented 40% of the group's total. Thus, Sizzler's bang for the buck was 1.625 Awareness Level Points for every dollar spent on advertising i.e., 65% divided by 40%. I made this same calculation for all restaurants in the study group and presented them in my chart in descending performance rank order. Here's the result of my analysis:

Restaurant Chain	Bang for the Buck 9/90--8/91	Restaurant Chain	Bang for the Buck 9/91--8/92
Denny's	6.70 to 1	Chevy's	6.37 to 1
Chevy's	6.20 to 1	Marie Calendar	5.25 to 1
Black Angus	3.44 to 1	Denny's	4.78 to 1
Marie Calendar	1.83 to 1	Red Lobster	3.80 to 1
Red Lobster	1.63 to 1	Black Angus	2.41 to 1
Sizzler	1.625 to 1	Sizzler	2.20 to 1

Restaurant Chains' Advertising Expenditure — Bang for the Buck

Thus, through this analysis, it was evident to me that Sizzler's advertising effectiveness had come in dead last for the previous two years when compared to its perceived closest competitors. What was really compelling, I thought, was that this conclusion was based on performance data provided by Dailey and Associates![32] I felt I had provided some very compelling evidence that our new advertising agency was not doing a credible job and that this should be a topic of serious discussion at the next Concept Committee meeting.

---

[32] Dailey & Associates took over Sizzler's account in early 1992. Thus, this analysis is as much an indictment of BBDO's performance as it is of their successor.

This matter was not placed on the agenda for the next meeting and I have no idea if my concerns were seriously discussed by Sizzler's senior management although I am aware that other franchisees were also questioning the wisdom of staying the course with our new agency. Eventually I resigned from this committee out of frustration with its inability to accomplish anything worthwhile and to disassociate myself from it for fear that by remaining on it I would be viewed by my peers as endorsing the things Sizzler was doing.[33]

Without regard for Sizzler's lack of interest in TQM concepts, I remained dedicated to the idea of developing a TQM culture within my own company and continued implement various TQM programs as quickly as my home study efforts allowed. I purchased a fairly sophisticated market research computer program used to developed, tabulate and analyze customer opinion questionnaires[34] and at any given time after that I had a customer opinion survey being conducted in one of my restaurants regarding some issue of interest. I also conducted a few customer focus groups in an attempt to understand how to improve our product and service.

One of the things I discovered from my own focus group research was that the idea in the customers' minds that Sizzler was a budget family steak house had not completely disappeared. It was evident that people still felt Sizzler was a place to enjoy a steak dinner and still wanted Sizzler to be a family budget steak house. From this I concluded that the right repositioning strategy for Sizzler was to return to its roots. I realized though that we could never go backward. Somehow, we had to move forward yet capture the essence of the restaurant's roots as a steak house.

With that idea in mind, I formed a Quality Improvement Project Team consisting of four of my company managers and assistant managers and together we talked, brainstormed and conducted customer research. The outcome of this project was the introduction of a new steak merchandising program. The basic idea being that we would have a two-tiered steak menu. We would continue to offer the various tri-tip steak and steak combination platters that were the mainstay of our entree menu however, we would add a second tier of premium steaks. This portion of the menu would feature top sirloin, New York Cut, T-Bone and filet mignon. But more than that, we would add some merchandising romance to these products by giving them their own *brand name,* an idea suggested by Ray Coen. In this way we would create the aura of quality and uniqueness to differentiate these steaks from Sizzler's standard fair. The brand name we hit upon was *Dakota Ranch Steaks.*

---

[33] Sizzler eventually dropped Dailey & Associates as their advertising agency in 1996. They switched over to Foote, Cone and Belding --the very same agency Hugh Duncan used to run.

[34] *SurvyPro* by Apian Software, Menlo Park, California. 1-800-237-4565

Beyond creating a new promotional angle through the introduction of our *Dakota Ranch Steak* program, there was a more subtle but much more strategic aim incorporated in it. That being to draw ourselves back toward our roots as a Budget Steak House through the attendant pricing policy we employed. Recall that Sizzler originally used a retail markup multiplier of around 2.1 to 2.5 times plate cost but had gradually moved up to a cost-to-retail multiplier of between 3 to 4 times plate cost for its entrees. The plan for our premium steaks was more or less to go back to the old multiplier. Actually, the plan was to price the product such that the Gross Profit dollars per serving was the same as or just slightly higher than the Gross Profit dollars per serving we were currently obtaining from our tri-tip steak platters and steak combination platters. For example, at that time, a typical Sizzler steak dinner or combination platter was retailing for between $7 and $9-- say $8 on average. Using an average markup multiplier of 3.5 this means that the average plate cost was around $2.30 thus our average Gross Profit per serving was around $5.70. If our plate cost for one of our premium *Dakota Ranch Steaks* was, say $4.25, then the retail price we would assign would be $4.25 plus $5.70 or $9.95. In effect, in this example, we were using a cost-to-retail markup of 2.34 times cost.[35]

Inherent in this strategy was the presumption that without regard to the increase this would have on the cost of goods sold on our financial statements as a percent of sales and therewith a decrease in profit as a percent of sales, there would be no negative affect on bottom line results in terms of dollars. We felt there was no downside to this program but, on the other hand, given the really substantial improvement in the price/value relationship of this product line, it appeared to us the potential for this innovation to entice many of our former loyal budget steak customers to come back was pretty good. Recall my comments regarding Vince Liuzza's strong appeal for Sizzler to return to its roots and get back in the neighborhood of around a 45% cost of goods sold—an overall 2.2 markup multiplier. Well, if the premium steak selections gained traction, it wouldn't take long to get the overall cost of goods sold as a percentage of sales revenue down close to 33%--a 3.0 markup multiplier or slightly below that with a *zero* reduction in gross profit dollars. If the premium steak program gained significant traction, our overall average markup multiplier would bring us back close to where we were in the nineteen sixties. Sales would increase, gross profit in dollars would increase and the consumers' perception of Sizzler as a budget steak house would rebound. Now, in my mind, *that's* a silver bullet.

---

[35] I often heard Mike Minchin refer to the restaurant business as a "penny business." What he meant by this was that the bottom-line profit, a restaurant operation earns is measured in pennies. For example, using the above Average Gross Margin per Customer of $5.70, once you factor in all the additional costs of serving that one meal the $5.70 Gross Margin must cover including hourly labor, management salaries, utilities, repairs and maintenance, advertising, insurance, rent, legal, accounting, income taxes, etc. the net cash to go into the owner's pocket from that one customer is a little less than fifty cents. Thus, a ten-cent swing in the cost to serve one customer will translate into a twenty percent swing in a restaurant's net profit if that one dime is multiplied times every customer served. In a typical Sizzler during the nineteen-eighties, an ability to increase the per customer profit margin by one penny for every customer served in one year would translate into approximately a $2,000 increase in the unit's annual pre-tax profit.

So, with that plan in mind, I had a new menu board made whereupon we prominently featured Dakota Ranch Steaks as a selection of premium steaks for the true steak lover. This idea caught on reasonably well and it was not below me to tell all the Sizzler franchisees in the Bay Area what I was up to. Within a fairly short time, there were several other Sizzler Franchisees in the Bay Area also merchandising Dakota Ranch Steaks. Soon enough, the Bay Area franchisee's renegade steak program caught the attention of Dick Birmingham and he immediately took action to stop the project. The word he put out was that no franchisee was allowed to merchandise anything other than approved Sizzler menu items and he would get a court order to restrain us from merchandising Dakota Ranch Steaks if he had to. This was a far cry from the days when Jack Williams was experimenting with his expanded salad bar and Denny Robertson's steak and all you can eat shrimp idea. But those were different times with different people running the show.

But the Dakota Ranch Steak program didn't end there. Dick Birmingham had that brand name protected as a Sizzler trademark and within less than a year, Sizzler was merchandising its familiar tri-tip steaks as Sizzler's Dakota Ranch Steaks throughout the country. Had the company embraced the product line of premium steaks along with the Dakota Ranch Steak brand name and pricing strategy, who is to say what would have resulted. Unfortunately, the decision was to not change anything about the steaks we were serving except the name and this approach ultimately proved not to have a significant effect on consumer perceptions of Sizzler or create a renewed desire for them to come back.

About the same time that I was working with my Dakota Ranch Steak project, Sizzler corporate had a test project of its own underway. Bob Zappelli was assigned to a special project in the Atlanta market along with Ray Coen. The basic idea behind Bob and Ray's project was to accomplish pretty much the same thing I was trying to accomplish in Santa Rosa, namely, reinvigorating the consumer's interest in Sizzler as a steak house rather than as an all-you-can-eat buffet restaurant. Ray Coen was already deeply familiar with Sizzler and with its problems because, if you recall, he had been Sizzler's Senior Account Representative first with Hall, Butler and Blatherwick and later with BBDO. By this time however, Ray had long since left BBDO but maintained an ongoing friendship with several Sizzler franchisees including myself and through these associations kept abreast of Sizzler's trials and tribulations.

In any case, together Bob Zappelli and Ray Coen went to work trying to develop their own repositioning strategy for Sizzler using all of the stores in Atlanta as their test site. They used the same brand name approach to merchandising steaks that I was using in Santa Rosa. They also used the same *Dakota Ranch Steak* brand name. The brand name idea belongs to Ray Coen. It was he who suggested it to me and I suggested it to my QUIP Team who, in turn named it the *Dakota Ranch Steak* project. They also tried some creative new approaches to merchandising Steak and Lobster. With the benefit of some additional funding for the creation of a medium budget television commercial along with some money to air the commercials on a limited basis, the results of their project were just short of phenomenal. In this lackluster market their project had managed to increase sales by 25% above sales for the same period in the prior year. Elated with the results of their efforts, Bob made an enthusiastic report to senior management that it appeared they had succeeded is developing a viable turn-around formula. With this, Dick Birmingham flew to Atlanta to take a look. His reaction to what he saw was definitely not what Bob Zappelli expected. Dick ordered that most of the changes to the test stores be undone, recommended a few new changes of his own and left town. Shortly thereafter, the sales in the Atlanta stores returned to their previous levels and Bob's test project was terminated.

I believe part of the reason for Dick's resistance to the changes made in the Atlanta project can be attributed to the fact that he was opposed to Sizzler's re-emergence as a steak house. I heard him make this statement on several occasions but the underlying reasons were never made clear. He held this opinion despite the fact that steak sales continued to be Sizzler's number one seller among those customers who ordered an entree as opposed to the Buffet Court. I can say unequivocally that this opinion was not based on any consumer research or a belief on Dick's part that American's appetite for steak was on a decline. In fact, in the midst of Sizzler's crisis, Dick took it upon himself to launch a new restaurant chain called the Buffalo Ranch Steak House. He said he was merely looking for a way to utilize some of Sizzler's excess properties in its over built markets, but the money invested in these new restaurants suggested something else. If all that Dick wanted to accomplish was to thin a market, he could have bought the company out of its leases. There is no doubt that this would have been an expensive proposition, but certainly less so than the $750,000 it was costing to convert excess Sizzlers into Buffalo Ranch Steak Houses. There has been some speculation that at least part of the impetus behind launching the Buffalo Ranch Steak House chain can be attributed to the rebuffing Dick Birmingham received from the senior management of the Outback Steak House chain. Dick approached that organization with the proposition of allowing Sizzler International to develop the Outback concept in Southern California but was flatly denied the opportunity. The folks at Outback told Dick they didn't think he was running a very good operation and, as the story goes, Dick felt compelled to teach them a lesson.

In addition to the money the company was investing in this new restaurant concept, Dick was also diverting the attention and energy of the marketing and product development staff towards his new concept as well. To my way of thinking, the launching of the Buffalo Ranch Steak House chain at a time when Sizzler was in so much trouble would be akin to using the cargo hold of a sinking ship as a workshop in which to build a new boat. As time would eventually prove, this was indeed the case. When Sizzler declared bankruptcy and closed 120 Sizzlers, it also closed all of its Buffalo Ranch Steak Houses.

The fundamental objective of the Atlanta repositioning strategy and of my Dakota Ranch Steak menu addition was to entice consumers away from the Buffet Court back to the entree menu. By this time, it was clear to both Bob Zappelli and myself and most other Sizzler franchisees that a Sizzler restaurant could never be profitable if its principal product was the Buffet Court with a fixed price of $5.99 at lunch and $6.99 at dinner. This product simply did not produce a sufficient gross margin per customer to cover the other variable costs, and support the fixed costs given the limited seating capacity of a Sizzler which, for the most part, ranged between 145 to 220 seats, nor attract enough customers. Moreover, Sizzler's food preparation and storage areas--i.e., the back of the house was designed to support a limited budget steak menu. Thus, the preparation and holding equipment as well as the dry and cold storage we had available for our buffet menu became a hodgepodge of convoluted, make-do working spaces, storage spaces and preparation procedures that was less that appropriate in all but the newest Sizzlers and just short of a nightmare for the older, smaller units.

With this in mind, in August, 1992 I sent a letter to Hugh Duncan suggesting that the only appropriate long-term strategy for the company was to pursue a marketing plan that would generate a higher average check. As a way to make my point, I provided him with an eight-year trend in our average check juxtaposed to the trend in the Consumer Price Index over the same time period. The point being to illustrate how much our average check would have to increase just to stay *even* with where we once were and where we would have to be to remain viable. Following is my analysis and Hugh Duncan's response:

February	CPI 1977=100	Annual % Change	Sizzler's Check Average	Annual % Change	
1985	173.5	/	$6.55	/	
1986	179.8	+3.6%	$6.81		+4.0%
1987	182.0	+1.2%	$6.69		-1.8%
1988	188.9	+3.8%	$7.05		+5.4%
1989	197.7	+4.7%	$7.47		+6.0%
1990	208.2	+5.3%	$7.39		-1.1%
1991	219.7	+5.5%	$7.01		-5.1%
1992	227.0	+3.3%	$7.18		+2.4%
TOTAL CHANGE		+30.8%*			+9.6%*

(*Error in sum of annual totals due to rounding)

From the above one can see that Sizzler's Average Check would have to be increased by $1.37 up to $8.57 just to reflect the changes in the Consumer Price Index. This much of an increase in a mid-scale restaurant's average check is enormous. Even assuming a superbly executed strategy it would probably require two to three years to successfully raise the average check this much. Keep in mind that although the average check was falling well behind parity with the Consumer Price Index, competitive forces plus occasional changes in the minimum wage law insured that labor costs more or less tended to keep up with this change and the CPI COLAS in our lease agreements insured that our facility occupancy costs would also tend to track with the CPI. My conclusion was that Sizzler *had* to develop a marketing strategy to reverse the trend in its declining average check or face certain financial disaster.

To Hugh Duncan, this message was just so much hyperbole. His response was that the appropriate strategy should be to generate higher sales volumes by *lowering* prices even more! The underlying assumption to this argument being that there would be a greater percentage increase in customers resulting from any given percentage decrease in menu prices. The fact that I had already tested this assumption in my Albuquerque Sizzler and that other franchisees had tried much the same thing--all to no avail seemed not to matter. Neither did the fact that the percentage increase in customers necessary to sufficiently offset lower prices and thereby yield an increase in profit would have to be far beyond what could reasonably be expected. For example, based on a simple breakeven analysis, I was able to demonstrate that if prices were lowered such that the average check declined by one dollar--from $7.25 to $6.25--approximately a fourteen percent decrease, customer counts would have to increase by more than *fifty-six* percent for this strategy to pass the breakeven point and produce an increase in unit cash flow.

Senior Sizzler management's feeling that lowering menu prices would be the road to our salvation at first appears even more perplexing considering the fact that in June, 1992 Hugh Duncan was quoted in *Nation's Restaurant News* that "the fundamental Sizzler Concept we had in the nineteen-eighties with the grill and the salad bar is the right concept for the nineteen-nineties We're gradually returning to that and concentrating on the basics." Mr. Duncan further went on to describe Sizzler's new trio of steaks featuring the New York cut, top sirloin and filet mignon with price points ranging between $8.99 and $10.99.[36] The upshot of this pronouncement was the development of a new TV commercial featuring the New York cut at $9.99.

This new commercial was aired in the San Francisco Bay Area for six weeks starting around July, 1992 and in Southern California plus other parts of the country more or less around the same time. Unfortunately, like so many of our previous Steak promotions, this one was a flop in that it did nothing to spur customer counts or sales. It appears to me that the failure of this one TV promotion to single handedly turn Sizzler around was deemed by senior management to be proof positive that Sizzler could not recapture its previous Budget Steak market niche nor increase its average check. I feel, that to make such a significant strategic decision based on the poor performance of one TV promotion was a mistake. I believe that had Sizzler made a concerted long-term effort to get back to basics the chain probably would have eventually recovered.

But that was not the course the company pursued. The fact of the matter is the company could not seem to stick to any one course. From nineteen ninety-two forward, senior

---

[36] *Nation's Restaurant News*, June 2, 1992 Volume 26, No. 6, p. 39

management remained lost and the resulting marketing programs, products and product pricing ideas descending from the top had no single strategic focus. In a bit of what I believe to be reasonably warranted sarcasm, I began referring to Sizzler's various marketing plans and strategies as its latest "Concept *de jour*." I have no idea whether or not this malady was a topic of debate between Dick Birmingham and Hugh Duncan or if it was, what different courses of action those two individuals advocated. However, in February, 1993, just one year after becoming President of Sizzler U.S.A., Hugh Duncan resigned citing "philosophical differences of opinion" with Dick Birmingham and Mr. Birmingham therewith reassumed the position of President and Chief Operating Officer of Sizzler Restaurants International.

With the failure of the Kids' Bar, Australian Baked Chicken, Sea Monsters, Dakota Ranch Steaks, the Atlanta Test, the New York cut promotion and a host of other product ideas to have any effect on Sizzler's declining sales and customer counts throughout nineteen ninety-two and nineteen ninety-three, Dick Birmingham felt compelled to try yet another new approach. Again, with a great deal of fanfare, a new, *new* repositioning of Sizzler was announced. This time the key element of the repositioning plan was to be price appeal. The intent was to offer an entirely new menu featuring a host of new products with menu prices ranging around five to six dollars. The products upon which this program was to be based were largely, precooked items to be reconstituted by boiling in a bag or oven heating or instant foods that could be reconstituted by adding hot water. With time as Sizzler's ever-present enemy, the company planned to rush this program into place in three of Sizzler's major markets: Baltimore/Washington D.C.; Phoenix and San Diego.

Although the new products were lackluster to say the least, what was really appalling about this program was the utter lack of thought given to the anticipated financial results. In Sizzler's January, 1994 edition of its News Letter *That Sounds Good* the new vision for the new, new repositioning was that customer counts were anticipated to increase from fifteen to twenty-five percent while the average check was expected to decrease by five to ten percent resulting in an expected increase in food cost of three to four points. Immediately upon receiving a copy of the newsletter with this announcement, I put pencil to paper and calculated the bottom line affect this program would achieve if actual results occurred as expected. The conclusion was frightening and I fired off a letter to Sizzler Headquarters to point this out.

In my letter I included a summary of my analysis in which I used actual performance data from one of my Sizzlers as the basis upon which to project the expected bottom-line results if all changes occurred as anticipated. Here is what I discovered:

	Actual Performance Results for January, 1994	Recast Results Assuming the minimum expected change occurs	Recast Results Assuming the maximum expected change occurs
Customer Count	13,875	15,956	17,343
Check Average	$7.25	$6.89	$6.53
Avg. hourly wage	$5.22	$5.22	$5.22
Labor Productivity	4.00	4.15	4.25
Gross Sales	$100,626	$109,937	$113,255
Food Cost	35%	38%	39%
Direct Labor	18%	18.25%	18.8%
Other Controllables	8.5%	7.5%	7.5%
Labor Overhead	5.75%	5.75%	5.75%
Manager Bonus	1.0%	1.0%	1.0%
Total Variable Costs	75.75%	79.00%	80.55%
Fixed Mgt Salaries	$6,000	$6,000	$6,000
Rent	$8,300	$8,300	$8,300
Other Fixed Costs	$2,700	$2,700	$2,700
Total Fixed Costs	$17,000	$17,000	$17,000
Cash Flow	$7,402	$6,087	$5,028

In the closing paragraph of my letter, I pointed out that under the assumption that customer counts increased by fifteen percent, check average decreased by five percent and food cost went up by three points, then unit cash flow would *decrease* eighteen percent and by assuming the best outcome of this new, new, repositioning that unit cash flow would *decrease* by thirty-two percent.

I sent copies of this letter to every Sizzler franchisee in the San Francisco Bay Area Advertising Cooperative in an effort to raise the level of awareness concerning the inadvisability of the company's latest concept repositioning strategy. I learned later that this letter was widely circulated among the senior management at Sizzler Headquarters.

In March, 1994 at an official Bay Area Advertising Co-op meeting in Daly City, I was approached by Wayne McDaniels, Sizzler's new Vice President of Operations[37] with the only response to my letter I ever received. He made a casual comment to me that there are other ways to interpret the numbers. With that the company went forward with the program as announced.

---

[37] The re-establishment of the position of Vice President of Operations occurred concurrently with Hugh Duncan's resignation.

Other ways to interpret the numbers indeed! I have no idea how senior Sizzler management interpreted the numbers; however, I strongly suspect that the projected results of the new repositioning strategy were based mostly on thin air, a hope and a prayer and that no serious analysis of the plan or research into consumer reaction to the new products was ever made. In any case, when Sizzler declared bankruptcy, it either closed or otherwise divested itself of all of its units in all three markets where this program was implemented.

By this time, one would think a certain ground swell of discontent and frustration with Sizzler leadership among the franchisees and Sizzler corporate employees as well would have become manifest. Be it in the form of a flood of letters and phone calls from franchisees to Jim Collins and/or the NSFA leadership demanding change, perhaps a law suit or two, letters to the press, or other assorted forms of protest, in whatever form such protests evolve, in some way or another one would think the exasperation with the turmoil in which the system had become embroiled should have erupted more or less spontaneously in the face of the organization. I think this probably would have happened were it not for one significant reason: e. coli. For with the e. coli disaster came another unwelcome guest which can best be described as *plausible deniability*. I could sense it and I'm sure many others could too. Whether one spoke with Jim Collins, Dick Birmingham, the senior marketing staff or the advertising agency executives, there was a common mantra they were all chanting and it was *e. coli*. That disaster, the negative effect of which were still being felt within Sizzler, afforded everyone in a position of responsibility for Sizzler's decline the opportunity to use it as a scapegoat for *all* Sizzler's problems. Of course, this just wasn't so however under these circumstances no one, including myself, felt bold enough to launch an attack on the company's leadership even though it was an action I had given some serious consideration. It was my feeling as I'm sure it must have been the feeling of anyone else who may have been considering launching an aggressive protest that the effort would fail and there would be some very unpleasant consequences in store for anyone making such an attack. Thus, at this critical time in Sizzler's life the revolt that might have been, never occurred and things only continued to get progressively worse.

Throughout the early nineteen-nineties, the NSFA Board of Trustees continued from time to time to encourage Dick Birmingham to lead the company in the develop of a Strategic Plan. By this time, it was evident that senior management was grasping at straws and some sense of stability and solid direction was desperately needed. The NSFA Board of Trustees made a suggestion to Dick that he at least explore the idea of formal Strategic Planning. This was something with which the NSFA Board was familiar because they had gone through the strategic planning process in nineteen ninety-nine, shortly after Jack Williams was retired. As an inducement for Dick to explore this idea, the NSFA offered to pay half the bill for Sizzler International to bring in a Strategic Planning management consultant to make a presentation.

Together, Sizzler International and the NSFA Board of Trustees engaged the services of a Strategic Plan Facilitator by the name of Reb Gooding who provided his services under the name Direction Associates which was headquartered in Indianapolis. Reb Gooding had substantial experience in leading the senior management of large corporations through the strategic planning process, had facilitated the development of the NSFA's strategic plan about four years earlier and was confident he could demonstrate how the process worked to Dick Birmingham and Jim Collins.

Dick agreed to explore the idea by conducting a two-day strategic planning working session. Reb Gooding made it clear that a company of Sizzler's size, complexity and circumstances could not develop a full-blown strategic plan in two days. The intent of the project was essentially to introduce the senior Sizzler management team to the process. So, with this understanding, a fairly large group of Sizzler's senior staff including Dick Birmingham and Jim Collins and several NSFA Trustees including myself convened for a two-day strategic planning demonstration exercise.

For the most part, this two-day affair went pretty much as one would expect. Reb Gooding led the group through a brain storming session wherein he helped us to verbalize Sizzler's major strengths, weaknesses, opportunities and threats as well as identify our Key Success Factors, define our customers, define their Key Buying Factors, formulate a Mission Statement, identify Objectives, Strategies, Goals and Action Plans. This was all done in a fairly superficial way of course, which was all that was possible given the time restraint and lack of research data needed to development a true strategic plan. Nevertheless, I thought the exercise accomplished its purpose which was to present the strategic planning process to senior management.

Unfortunately, Dick Birmingham was unimpressed. He was so unimpressed in fact that he refused to pay Sizzler International's half of Direction Associates' bill for the two-day affair. Instead, Dick forwarded the bill to the National Sizzler Franchisee Association who then paid the entire ten thousand dollars. This event marked the last real effort of the NSFA Board of Trustees to work as a body in a cooperative effort with SRI to help the company solve its problems.

A few months prior to this Strategic Planning working session I was approached informally and confidentially by a mid-level executive in Sizzler's marketing department with what can best be described as a plea for help. It was this individual's belief, or perhaps hope may be a better word, that the NSFA Board of Trustees could approach Jim Collins on behalf of all the stake holders in Sizzler and persuade him to remove Dick Birmingham as the company's President. As this individual put it, morale among the headquarters staff was already extremely low and declining fast. She went on to say that the employees who worked out of Corporate Headquarters were afraid to venture out of their respective offices for fear of running into Dick Birmingham in the elevator or hall way where upon he would inevitably find some reason to verbally pounce on the hapless individual for whatever reason happened to be handy at that moment. Unbeknownst to this executive, I was already well aware of the declining morale problem among the headquarters staff. By this time, Dick's reputation for exhibiting a Jekyll-and-Hyde behavior toward his subordinates had pretty much become common knowledge. In fact, on two separate occasions, I had two Corporate Vice Presidents express the feeling to me that Dick had ruined their life. Based on the reports and gossip emanating from corporate headquarters it sounded to me like Dick Birmingham's leadership style consisted of three principal elements: intimidation, humiliation and revenge.

It's likely that other NSFA Trustees had received similar pleas for help but, alas to no avail and for good reason, or better said, clear reason. By this time, Ron Higgins, formerly a silent investing partner in FORBCO had become the managing partner following the dismissal of Jack Williams and also inherited the position of President of the NSFA. As it happens, while all of this turmoil was going on, Ron was in secret negotiations with Dick Birmingham to sell all of FORBCO's Sizzler to the franchisor and would never have agreed to pass these appeals onto Jim Collins. I learned this fact from Tom Gregory, a year or so later, well after his departure from Sizzler of course.

My perception of Dick's leadership style can best be described as the Lone Ranger Paradigm. That is to say that he perceived himself as a hero, astride a white horse, six shooters in hand with a gun belt loaded with silver bullets and his mission was to single handedly ride into harm's way and save the day. Dick clearly believed his mission was to *get results and get them fast*. I believe this entrepreneurial leadership approach wherein it is the Chief Executive's job to get results works well in smaller organizations during their early developmental stages however as an organization grows in size and complexity, I think the role of the Chief Executive must evolve into one wherein his job is to *build a management team, organizational structure, systems and culture that gets results*. Sizzler had long since evolved into a sufficiently large and complex organization needing that kind of leadership yet, Dick Birmingham, in my opinion, was never a team builder, nor much of an organizational architect. Prior to the aforementioned Strategic Planning demonstration project, I asked Dave Barrows for a copy of the company's Organization Chart. He said none existed because Dick Birmingham didn't believe in them.

However, out of deference for this executive's appeal to me for help I took it upon myself to make an effort to do something. It was obvious that any attempt to approach Dick Birmingham directly regarding his loss of respect among his subordinates would be futile. So, I hit upon the idea of suggesting to Dick that the company measure it's over all management performance against the standards of management excellence established in the Malcolm Baldrige National Quality Award criteria.[38] I avoided any discussion about specific measurement standards but suggested instead that, given the significant role unit level performance audits had come to play in Sizzler's organizational management system and culture, a logical extension of that corporate culture would be to subject the total organization, including senior management, to a performance audit. As I made this suggestion, I was aware that the first issue put under study by the Baldrige Award criteria was the quality of Organizational Leadership. My hidden agenda being of course, that should Dick pursue this suggestion, the weaknesses in his leadership style would become evident to both himself and the Board of Directors and hopefully corrected. My expectation that this plan would work as I hoped was not great. A later event would demonstrate, this expectation was quite realistic.

Moreover, beyond my specific hidden agenda, I felt that such an audit would enable Dick Birmingham, Jim Collins and the entire Board of Directors to acquire an improved understanding of the company's strengths and weaknesses and therewith enable them to begin to forge the organization into one better equipped to deal with its many challenges. Needless to say, my suggestion went nowhere. Indeed, my suggestion became something of a joke to Dick Birmingham and he managed to degrade it into a silly suggestion for the company to divert its attention away from an attempt to re-acquire an ability to effectively compete in the market place to an attempt to win some useless trophy. The fact that over a million organizations throughout the world have availed themselves of the Baldrige Award criteria, not so much to see if they can win the trophy but to better understand what it now takes for an organization to maintain a sharp competitive edge was completely beyond Dick Birmingham. To him, my suggestion was nothing but a stupid idea and he was more than willing to share that feeling with me and everyone else in our strategic planning group.

Besides aggravating his subordinates, Dick Birmingham also managed to aggravate many Sizzler franchisees, albeit not in a significant way, but nevertheless in a way that was a very unbecoming example of a leader's self-serving attempt to avoid the same sacrifices the organization he purports to lead must suffer. Some years earlier, Dick obtained a special dispensation from the Board of Directors to be exempted from a corporate policy that prohibited Sizzler International employees from having any ownership interest in a franchised Sizzler. Indeed, one of Sizzler's former Vice Presidents was summarily fired when it was discovered he had clandestinely acquired a partnership interest in a multi-

---

[38] The Malcolm Baldrige National Quality Award program was established by an act of Congress in 1987. The program is administered by the National Institute of Standards and Technology which is an agency within the U.S. Department of Commerce. The award was named after Malcolm Baldrige, President Regan's Secretary of Commerce who was killed in a horseback riding accident in 1987. The mission of this program is to promote the improvement in the production of quality products and services through the improvement in organizational management practices. Each year, three U.S. companies--a manufacturing company, a service company and a small business--are presented the award by the President at a White House ceremony. The award is based on the total points each contestant achieves in seven audit categories. There are one thousand points possible and to be in contention for the award, an award applicant needs to achieve a score generally above eight hundred. During the first pass through the audit format, the typical "well-run company" usually scores below two hundred.

unit franchised Sizzler company. Despite the corporation having terminated a Vice President for violating corporate policy regarding the prohibition of Sizzler International management also being a Sizzler Franchisee, Dick Birmingham was allowed to put his wife Martha and his two sons into business as the owner/operators of a franchised Sizzler. This action did not reflect favorably on Dick among senior management but evidently, he was oblivious to this fact.

The final insult to the franchisee community came after the Board of Directors established a new policy that the company would not, under any circumstances, purchase any Sizzler restaurants a franchisee wished to sell. This practice had for years been acceptable when the location and selling price of a franchised Sizzler met the franchisor's acquisition criteria. However, by nineteen ninety-four the official position of the company was that it did not want to assume any additional business or financial risk through the acquisition of franchised Sizzlers due to the difficult times the company was experiencing. I know this to be the case because my offer to sell my units to the company was declined on this basis. However, despite this official corporate position, the Board of Directors agreed to purchase Martha Birmingham's money losing Sizzler. That this action was taken with some sort of strings attached requiring Dick to reimburse Sizzler International for any financial loss from the acquisition is almost certain although I have no way of knowing if this was the case. For Sizzler International to buy back Martha Birmingham's Sizzler without such conditions is difficult to imagine considering the board of directors' which included Dick Birmingham fiduciary and legal responsibility to put the financial interests of the company's stockholders ahead of their own personal interests or the personal interests of a particular board member.

By mid- nineteen ninety-four my opinion of Sizzler's future was bleak to say the least. Dick Birmingham announced his resignation from Sizzler as its President and Chief Executive Officer on June 30, 1994. What he left behind was a company in shambles. Sales and customer counts were declining faster than ever, the company had no real direction, the senior management team he and Hugh Duncan had assembled was nowhere near qualified to turn the company around, and the morale of virtually all of Sizzler's employees and franchisees were at an all-time low. The Board of Trustees of the Sizzler National Franchise Association had pretty much thrown in the towel insofar as any belief that they could contribute to a turnaround effort.

The people in charge of corporate restaurant operations, especially at the unit management level--were frustrated and exhausted from an unending string of repositioning efforts that led nowhere. Moreover, the array of new products which had been introduced over the last several years had created a chaotic condition in the restaurants which were never designed or equipped to properly prepare many of them. And of course, it goes without saying that Dick's departure was not preceded by any serious transition planning.

Why the Board of Directors allowed this collapsing of the organization to go on month after month without any intervention is beyond belief. It's not as though they had no inkling of the havoc Dick Birmingham was creating. Its altogether likely that Jim Collins was approached frequently with admonitions about the failings of his Chief Executive. I am aware of several such warnings and have in my possession a copy of a letter given to Jim Collins but addressed to Jose Arau, the Principal Investment Officer of the California Public Employees Retirement System pleading for him to intercede in Sizzler's affairs on behalf of his fund's investors' ownership interest in Sizzler--something CALPERS was known to do from time to time. I do not know whether or not Mr. Arau received the letter but if so, evidently CALPERS had an insufficient investment in Sizzler to warrant that organization flexing its muscle, if indeed, it had any ownership interest in Sizzler at all.

I am also aware that Mr. Edward Sheldrake, the owner of another restaurant chain in Southern California and confidant of Jim Collins warned Jim that Dick was ruining his company. If this were not enough, an article appeared in *Restaurant Institutions* citing a joint *R&I* and HVS Executive Search firm study which evaluated the pay relative to performance for seventy-five publicly traded restaurant company CEOs in the country. Of all the CEO's evaluated, Dick Birmingham appeared on the list second from the bottom. Despite all these warnings, pleadings and journalistic evaluations, Jim Collins and the rest of the Board of Directors remained steadfast in their support of Dick Birmingham until he resigned.

Dick Birmingham's resignation as Chief Executive Officer of Sizzler Restaurants International did not end his influence on the organization however. He was immediately installed as the company's newest Outside Director. A place was made for him by the Board's decision to remove its Vice Chairman—Tom Gregory. Vince Liuzza made the comment to me that that made perfect sense to him--after all, Tom Gregory was the only Director on the Board that even knew how to spell 'Restaurant'. One of Dick's first official acts as a director, was to vote on his own previous recommendation that Kevin Perkins, the man in charge of the Australian market, be promoted to President of Sizzler International.

Although Kevin Perkins' track record in Australia, from all indications, was impeccable the fact remained that he was experienced at presiding over the operation of only thirty-nine Sizzlers in a market where the Sizzler concept was still well received by the consuming public and the employees worked under an entirely different set of labor laws, an entirely different pay scale and probably a different work ethic as well. Moreover, the principal focus of Mr. Perkins' job and substance of his experience was in executing a defined restaurant concept whereas what Sizzler most needed at this time was someone experienced in defining the concept to be executed. Add to this the fact that Kevin Perkins was not well connected in the U.S., had no outside associates whom he could tap for senior management positions in Sizzler and therefore no real team building opportunities. To me and to many other franchisees it appeared the recommendation of

Kevin Perkins as Sizzler's new CEO was not a good idea. Add to this the fact that Dick Birmingham's track record at selecting senior management personnel for Sizzler was, shall we say, less than stellar. One would think that Jim Collins and the rest of the Board of Directors would have given these facts some serious thought considering the company's ongoing problems.

In any case, Ron Higgins, along with Robert Minshew, Jr., Vice President of the NSFA and Mike Lonegan, a former Trustee whom altogether represented the three most influential franchisees in Sizzler met with Jim Collins and pointed these facts out to him quite thoroughly. Mike Lonegan recalls the meeting vividly. "We met in the Grill Room at the Vintage Country Club in Indian Wells California," Mike explained to me. "At this meeting we formally requested that any serious consideration of Kevin Perkins as Sizzler International's new CEO be done so after a nationwide search was conducted to find out who else in this country might be available to lead Sizzler's turnaround effort." The request simply put was for the Board of Directors to provide themselves with a slate of one or two additional candidates and make their selection of Sizzler's new Chief Executive within that context. Soon after this request, Jim Collins announced that Kevin Perkins was Sizzler's new Chief Executive Officer.

About six months prior to Kevin Perkins' promotion to Chief Executive Officer, Sizzler Restaurants International, the company engaged several consulting firms to help them develop yet another repositioning strategy. Presumably by this time, senior management had come to the realization that they lacked the talent necessary to stage a comeback on their own so they formed a sort of committee of consulting firms--each no doubt with a unique specialty--to help them out. The consultants conducted the obligatory consumer research and came to the conclusion that Sizzler's best bet was to try to re-establish itself as a mid-scale Steak and Seafood restaurant as opposed to a Buffet Restaurant with an average check somewhere between eight and ten dollars. I have no idea whether or not the fact that this was what most of the system's franchisees had been saying for years occurred to the Board of Directors. It appears that when such advice was given free, the value the board placed on it reflected its cost, which is to say they considered it worthless. However, when the same advice came with a price tag in excess of a million dollars, they thought it was pretty good.

Thus, when Kevin Perkins took hold of Sizzler's reins, the development of what was hoped to be Sizzler's final repositioning effort was just getting under way. The fundamental elements of the plan were already taking shape. Sizzler's new name would be Sizzler American Grill. Sizzler's nineteen ninety-five Annual Report made a very big deal of this project and they were clearly pinning their hopes on the success of this effort. The new menu would feature steaks, seafood--and something new for Sizzler--smoked ribs and chicken which were to be smoked daily in new equipment retrofitted into each unit specifically for that purpose. A new company logo featuring a new color scheme was developed along with a redecorated interior. Modifications to the wall-hung menu display were made as well along with the introduction of glossy hand-held menus customers could look at while waiting in line to order. The prevailing feeling at Sizzler's headquarters regarding the early progress was exuberant. This time, there was a belief that things were finally going to begin changing for the better.

I had my doubts and given the fact that the new management had once again opened the door to buying franchised Sizzlers, I sold my last two remaining stores to them and therewith ended my twenty-two-year career as a Sizzler Franchisee.[39]   Having made the mistake of rolling out the Buffer Court repositioning program too fast, this time Sizzler management was determined not to make the same mistake twice. This time management wanted to know beyond a shadow of a doubt that Sizzler American Grill was indeed, their silver bullet. With this objective in mind, the company proceeded to invest several million dollars renovating various units around the country to see if this new idea would work. It was made clear that this was a test and not a roll-out.

With that, the new concept was tested, modified, tested and modified again from its inception in nineteen ninety-five until the spring of nineteen ninety-seven! For *three years* the entire focus of the company's turnaround effort was invested in developing this one idea. During this period Kevin Perkins resigned as Sizzler's President and assumed the solitary title of Chief Executive Officer--just as Dick Birmingham had done--and Timothy Ryan, one of Sizzler's cadre of management consultants and former Taco Bell Vice President, was installed as Sizzler's President. It was under Mr. Ryan's leadership that the company declared bankruptcy. It was also Mr. Ryan's decision to dismantle the System Operation Support Department despite the pleading no to do so by Robert Minshew, Jr., by this time the NSFA's President. But dismantle the S. O. S. Department he did and replaced nearly all the remaining members of Sizzler's senior management staff with people of his own choosing.

The American Grill test continued on but with growing suspicions among the franchisees that it was not going well. Senior management refused to make known the results of the

---

[39] Unfortunately for me, the deal I made to sell the Sizzler I owned in the Plaza North Shopping Center in Petaluma California to Sizzler International fell apart because the landlord, Dr. Sayers, reneged on an initial indication that there would be no increase in rent upon assignment of my lease to Sizzler. At that time, I was paying approximately one hundred thousand dollars a year in rent including CAM and Dr. Sayers insisted that Sizzler agree to pay an additional nine thousand dollars a year--a feature the lease assignment clause allowed him to require. Sizzler refused and the deal died. I therewith closed the restaurant and Dr. Sayers agreed to let me off the lease if I gave him all the equipment in the restaurant which was showing a book value of around one hundred thousand dollars but had a liquidation value of more like fifteen thousand dollars. Within a few months of this event, Dr. Sayers approached Sizzler International directly and offered to lease that building to them for something less than what he had initially demanded and presumably sell them the all the equipment in the restaurant as well. In other words, it appeared he was trying to make more for himself by taking my equipment and cutting me out of the deal. Sizzler passed on this offer and as a result the former Petaluma Sizzler sat vacant for nearly two years. Ultimately, Dr. Sayers pulled all that equipment out of the building, invested a substantial sum of money to renovate the interior and divide it up into two smaller retail spaces (one of which has still not been leased as of May, 1998). Altogether, this ill-fated maneuver probably ended up costing him close to a half a million dollars—all in an attempt to make an extra nine thousand dollars a year. Oops!

test and ultimately the bankruptcy court appointed Franchisee Committee sued Sizzler in an attempt to get to the bottom of the test's progress. The information provided this committee was done so with the understanding that the committee members would hold it in strictest confidence and to the best of my knowledge, this commitment was honored. However, within a few months of this disclosure, the Sizzler American Grill test was declared "not viable."

In December, 1996 Timothy Ryan resigned as Sizzler's President and Kevin Perkins temporarily reassumed that position in addition to his title of Chief Executive Officer. Shortly after this organizational change, Mr. Perkins returned permanently to Australia. Thus, the office of Sizzler's President and Chief Executive Officer became detached from the body of the organization and re-situated nine thousand miles away. Christopher Thomas was given the title of Chief Operating Officer in addition to his title of Chief Financial Officer and the day-to-day management reins were once again handed off to someone else.

By this time Sizzler's official public position was that despite the problems the company is having with the concept in the United States, it is a strong competitor in all the foreign countries where it operates. Based on public pronouncements, it appears Sizzler is substantially predicating its ability to save itself on the performance of its foreign operations. However, this belief notwithstanding, in February, 1997 Sizzler's largest foreign franchisee, the Jardine-Matheson Company, owner/operator of thirty-nine Sizzlers in Australia, canceled all their Sizzler franchise agreements and announced they would close all of their Sizzlers in nineteen ninety-seven. Yet, to quote Kevin Perkins reaction to this event, "We expect that this development will have no impact on Sizzler's growth and development plans in the Asia Pacific region and minimal impact this fiscal year on Sizzler International's financial performance and results."[40]

In May, 1997 two of Sizzler's long time Directors, Wayne Kees and William Hansen retired and two new Directors, Robert A. Muh and Phillip D. Mathews were appointed to the Board. Dick Birmingham resigned from the board in February, 1996 and was replaced by Carol A. Scott, Ph.D. Professor of Marketing, UCLA. Although Sizzler's new directors had extensive successful experience in their respective fields, none had any multi-unit restaurant operation experience. Kevin Perkins was removed as Sizzler International's Chief Executive Officer and reassumed his role as President of Sizzler's foreign operations and Christopher Thomas was promoted to President and Chief Executive Officer of Sizzler's domestic operations. Jim Collins stepped in to assume the role of Chief Executive Officer of Sizzler International in addition to his ongoing role as Chairman of the Board.

[40] Market Guide News, http://www.makretguide.newsalert.com, 4/13/97

On June 2, 1997 the U.S. Bankruptcy Court for the Central District of California approved the financial reorganization plans of Sizzler International Inc., and its domestic subsidiary, Sizzler Restaurants International. Sizzler has presented plans to repay all of its creditors in full which amounted to approximately $95 million. The plan calls for $25 million in debts to be secured and paid from domestic operations and $70 million in debt to be secured and paid primarily with revenue from international operations. Combined, the plans call for repayment of this sum, paid in installments with interest over four to five years. Some of this money will come from the liquidation of excess operating equipment and real estate however the lion's share must, of necessity, come from future operating profits.

Of course, the sixty-four-dollar question now is will Sizzler survive and meet its debt obligations? The fact that the company emerged from Chapter 11 Bankruptcy at all is remarkable. Less than eighteen percent of the companies that file for Chapter 11 successfully reorganize and exit Chapter 11 as a going concern. Yet, of that eighteen percent that do emerge from Chapter 11, approximately fifty percent fail within the following twelve months.[41]

Sizzler launched its newly reorganized company with a marketing campaign founded in sweeping menu changes and initially featuring a new nine-item line of hamburgers to replace its previous four-item line of burgers.[42] In October, 1997 the company launched a promotional campaign dubbed 'the smart, new choice for steak lovers,' featuring a 1 lb. T-bone steak, a 14-ounce Rib Eye Steak, a 12-ounce New York cut, a ½ lb. Filet Mignon and a ½ lb. Top Sirloin. Citing the recent successes of higher-scale steak brands and the nation's resurgent appetite for beef, Christopher Thomas said "exploitation of the industry's red-meat renaissance really hasn't been done in the budget steak houses which recently have opted to pursue the buffet' route."[43] I could only smile at how familiar this change to its menu mimicked my *Dakota Ranch Steak* project which Dick Birmingham squelched in nineteen ninety-two.

However, at this point, I believe it's going to take more than adding five hamburgers and a line of premium steaks to the menu to reverse Sizzler's fortunes. But no matter what actions Sizzler takes, given its post-bankruptcy debt burden, the world will know soon enough if the company and its senior management has what it takes.

This then is the history of the Sizzler Restaurants International as I view it. What the future holds in store for the restaurant chain is something upon which I will not speculate.

---

[41] The Art of M & A: A Merger and Acquisition Buyout Guide by Stanley Foster Reed and Alexandra Reed Lajoux (The McGraw-Hill Companies, Inc., 1989 & 1995) p. 718.

[42] *Nation's Restaurant News*, June 16, 1997

[43] *Nation's Restaurant News*, November 24, 1997

Given the track record of Jim Collins and Sizzler's Board of Directors I will leave it up to the reader to draw his or her own conclusions. However, it is my hope that the company will survive and reemerge as a strong player in the mid-scale restaurant chain industry.

It is also my hope that this history can in some way be of value to those who are responsible for the leadership of their own organizations and valuable as well to any organization's managers, franchisees and investors. I believe there are many lessons that can be learned from Sizzler's decline and that is the subject to which I shall now turn.

Chapter 6
Lessons Learned

In the beginning was the plan.

And then came the assumptions
And the assumptions were without form.
And the plan was completely without substance,
And darkness was upon the face of the workers.
And they spake unto their marketing manager, saying,
> "it is a pot of crap, and it stinketh."

And the marketing manager went unto the strategists and sayeth,
> "It is a pile of dung, and none may abide the odor thereof."

And the strategists went unto the business managers and sayeth unto them,
> "It is a container of excrement, and it is very strong,
> such that none may abide by it."

And the business managers went unto the director and sayeth unto him,
> "It is a vessel of fertilizer, and none may abide its strength."

And the director went unto the vice president and sayeth,
> "It contains that which aids plant growth, and it is very strong."

And the vice president went unto the senior vice president and sayeth,
> "It promoteth growth, and it is powerful."

And the senior vice president went unto the president and sayeth unto him,
> "This powerful new plan will actively promote the growth and efficiency of the
> company and the business in general."

And the president looked upon the plan and saw that it was good…

And the plan became policy.[44]

When asked how he figured out that a Lithium Filament electrified in a vacuum would create light, Thomas Edison is quoted as saying that he did so by trying ten thousand other approaches first that didn't work. The point of course is that in the pursuit of successful new product ideas, it often must be preceded by a multitude of false starts and out and out unsuccessful efforts.

From over twenty years of personal observation and study, I feel it's safe to say that *every* company comes up with new product or service ideas from time to time that ultimately prove not to be viable. Developing new products or improving existing products in ways

---

[44] Leonard D. Goodstein, Timothy M. Nolan & J. William Pfeiffer, *Applied Strategic Planning*, Pfeiffer & Company, Copyright 1992, p. *vi.*

that create sustainable incremental sales is, by its nature, a trial-and-error process no matter how sophisticated a company's marketing research capabilities may be. Thus, I feel it is completely inappropriate and unreasonable to criticize Sizzler management for suggesting the Buffet Court repositioning idea. Neither Sizzler management nor the management of any company deserves to be criticized for testing novel ideas. That's part of their job.

My thesis throughout this book has been that the Buffet Court repositioning fiasco is really only a symptom of the reasons why the Sizzler Restaurant chain collapsed. I think the collapse was brought about by a combination of two fundamental debilitating weaknesses that together conspired to ruin the company which were a failure to develop effective Command and Control methods, systems and structure and an incorrect strategic focus

Sizzler management's' greatest fundamental mistake was in its failure to develop Management Command and Control methods, systems and structure capable of appropriately supporting the size and complexity of the company they had built. I know I have been especially critical of Dick Birmingham's management style which I characterized as the Lone Ranger Paradigm. But, to a significant degree, Dick was pretty much following in the footsteps of Tom Gregory and Mike Minchin in this regard. Considered together as the co-leaders of the company throughout the nineteen-eighties, those two individuals also pretty much called all the shots--and from what I saw I believe they called them based, for the most part, on their assessment of short-term system wide financial performance, personal observation, gut feel and anecdotal performance data.

As I have already pointed out, Sizzler never in its history engaged in a state-of-the-art strategic planning process. Sizzler never established a market research department or, I do not believe, otherwise developed the capability to systematically and effectively analyze consumer opinions of itself or its competitors, at least prior to the Buffet Court disaster. Sizzler most certainly never learned how to effectively determine the *incremental* sales generating capacity of new products nor fully appreciate *all* the incremental costs associated with an expanding and/or constantly changing menu.

Sizzler never learned how to effectively analyze the unit performance data it so painstakingly gathered and therewith develop the capability to differentiate between and appropriately address systemic operational problems and unit-specific problems. If Sizzler's approach to site selection methodology ever evolved beyond the "check list" technique it was one of the best kept secrets in the company. Additionally, I am certain that the marketing arm of the company, namely Product Development and Advertising including the advertising agency, had virtually no clue as to how difficult it had become for the unit level management and staff to execute the merchandising concept they had created. In fact, I'm not even sure that senior *Operations Management* was aware of how difficult it had become for unit level managers to execute the concept. With the exception of the Sizzler Salad Bar and Steak and All-You-Can-Eat Shrimp, Sizzler never established a systematic or organized means by which to identify and institutionalize some of the creative ideas developed by franchisees who certainly had a lot to contribute.

I am not sure; however, I doubt Sizzler management ever developed the capability to adequately evaluate the effectiveness of its advertising. The reason I am not sure of this probable weakness is that inherent in the franchising industry is a need, to a significant degree justified, for the franchisor to withhold from its franchisees knowledge it may have of the relative ineffectiveness of its advertising expenditures if such is the case. For example, in the late nineteen-eighties I was contributing approximately $420,000 a year to Sizzler's Bay Area Advertising Cooperative and its National Advertising Fund. (This is *in addition to* my annual franchise royalty payments of approximately $250,000). There were other Sizzler franchisees in the San Francisco Bay Area and Southern California contributing substantially more than I was. It doesn't take much imagination to see how tumultuous the franchisor/franchisee relationship would likely become if we were advised that the results we were getting from our advertising fund contributions were anything less than the best in the market as determined by an objective comparison of Sizzler and Sizzler's competitors' advertising efforts. Yet, try as one might to be the best, only one competitor in any given market at any given time can be number one in the various terms by which advertising efforts are measured and evaluated such as research data on aided and unaided recall, Top of Mind Awareness, effective media buying, etc. It's both impractical and potentially very harmful for both the franchisor and the franchisees to change advertising agencies frequently or even threaten to do this. However, this would almost certainly be the central topic of discussion and object of franchisee demands if ongoing, independent studies of the relative effectiveness of competitive advertising efforts revealed to franchisees that they weren't getting more for their money than anyone else.

This caveat to the issue of determining the effectiveness of advertising notwithstanding, it is still incumbent on the franchisor to make that determination. In Sizzler's case, this was done by the advertising agency as an adjunct to its primary role of developing creative advertising and placing it in the right places at the right times. It should come as no surprise that not once in my twenty-two years as a Sizzler owner did I ever witness an advertising agency presentation whereat the agency's spokesperson stood up and said, "Yeh, we screwed up. The product we selected to advertise was wrong, the story board was not sufficiently creative or compelling, we set the wrong price on the product and we put it in the wrong mediums at the wrong times and we paid too much for the time slots and space we bought. Sorry." If, on occasion the results of an ad campaign made recognition of one or more of those mistakes obvious to everyone, the agency always had the last word: "Well, what can you expect, considering the advertising budget we have to work with?" Add to this the fact that the advertising effort in regions (ADIs) which were comprised of both corporate owned and franchised units was conducted under the aegis of an Advertising Cooperative, where the group voted on what product to promote and at what price. Even though the product and pricing options available to members of the various advertising cooperatives around the country were pre-selected by senior Sizzler management and/or the advertising agency, there was always the final retort to any to any franchisee criticism of advertising effectiveness that we all 'voted' on it. To which I replied on more than one occasion that that was sort of like voting for President in Russia.

Almost always part of every advertising agency presentation was a demonstration of how good a job they were doing. Recall my discussion on this topic in Chapter 5 and the Bang for The Buck chart I developed and sent to the Concept Committee wherein I demonstrated that Sizzler came in dead last in the effectiveness of its efforts relative to selected competitors. Not only Dailey and Associates but, it seemed to me, Sizzler as well was quite put off by my analysis. The one lesson I have concluded from this exercise is that all efforts to assess the effectiveness of advertising *must* be made by someone other than the advertising agency even though the decision of whether or not to share the outcome of that analysis with the franchisees is admittedly problematic

Considering the number of operating units in Sizzler by nineteen ninety-two, the geographic dispersion of those units and the complexity of the merchandising concept along with the other weakness outlined above, I believe the system overall out grew the command-and-control systems Sizzler senior management employed. By the time Dick Birmingham stepped in as President of Sizzler, I truly believe senior management had lost control of the company. I strongly suspect, however, that most of senior management and the Board of Directors were unaware that they had lost control although I think that even if Dick Birmingham was also unaware of this fact when he took over the reins, he realized it soon enough.

Even though I now believe that by the time Dick Birmingham took over day-to-day management of Sizzler, the system's ultimate collapse was probably inevitable or at a minimum a cessation of growth and some contraction was inevitable. This fact, however, does not exempt him from responsibility for the unfortunate chain of events. He was, after all, the company's Chief Executive Officer and had been so for six years. Instead of focusing so much money and so much of his energy into the quest for new growth vehicles, over the preceding six years, I think he should have focused the majority of those resources on nurturing and reinforcing the company's existing operations.

Thus, first the strategic mistake Sizzler made was in focusing most, if not all of their energy and resources into increasing the number of operating units and the variety of products offered for sale in those units along with a quest for new growth vehicles while assuming the organizational structure, management systems, programs, procedures and processes they had established initially in the nineteen-seventies would adequately serve the company as it grew more complex.

In today's world, the life span of new products is so short and/or so easily copied by the competition that in-and-of-themselves, the development of new products generally does not offer a significant opportunity to gain a meaningful or lasting competitive advantage —certainly not in the restaurant business. Nowadays, I believe the arena in which successful companies will acquire their key competitive advantage is in the assimilation of more effective management systems. Indeed, in a study completed by the Massachusetts Institute of Technology in nineteen ninety, the conclusion reached into an investigation of why American businesses have lost such a significant share of the Gross World Product over the last half of this century is substantially attributable to the relatively ineffective management systems employed in this country as compared to what is occurring throughout the rest of the world—especially the Far East.[45]

I think the admonition offered CEOs in Michael Hammer and James Champy's Book *Reengineering the Corporation* fairly well sums up my first criticism of senior Sizzler management when they state:

> Some people think American companies would bounce back if only they had the right products and services for the times. We reject that thinking, because products have limited life spans, and even the best soon become obsolete. It is not products but the processes that create products that bring companies long-term success. Good products don't make winners; winners make good products.[46]

When one is at the top of one's form, when a company is the leader in its industry or at least its segment of an industry as Sizzler certainly was by the mid to late nineteen-eighties, it's hard to see the danger or even know of the dangers that the future holds in store. Market leadership and rapid growth pose their own unique kinds of business risk. There may be additional risks in market leadership of which I am unaware, but insofar as Sizzler is concerned, this is what I have observed:

The biggest risk is inherent in the fact that every day the company must plow new ground where no one has gone before. There are no benchmarks against which to assess the wisdom of your current course; no competitors to pursue or emulate; no mistakes of predecessors which, through their example, you know to avoid.

There is the risk of believing you're invincible; that so long as you keep on doing what you've been doing, you'll remain in the winner's circle.

---

[45] M. Detouzous, R. Lester and R. Solow, *Made in America: Regaining the Productivity Edge.* Cambridge, MA. The Massachusetts Institute of Technology, Commission on Industrial Productivity, Copyright by MIT Press, 1990.

[46] Michael Hammer & James Champy, *Reengineering the Corporation*, Harper Business, Copyright 1993, p. 24

There is the risk in being the leader because that's the company whose market everyone else in the industry most wants to attack and whose strategies they most want to copy. This in turn compels management to try and innovate at an exponential rate to stay ahead of the pack and in so doing, rush products to market and institute new strategies without proper testing and evaluation.

There is the risk of excessive negative media attention when something goes awry.

Ultimately, the various weaknesses in Sizzler's command and control systems and those unique threats which beset a market leader conspired to bring about a collapse. What could the company have done to avoid these dangers? What can *any* company do to avoid these dangers? The one thing I can now state with unequivocal certainty is very little other than retreat and downsize or let nature have its way once these problems begin to overwhelm the organization. Sizzler chose the high road and opted to retreat and downsize. Their decision to declare Chapter 11 bankruptcy while they were still financially viable was really the best of the two options available. The other was to stay the course and hope they could somehow muddle through. There is no doubt in my mind that had the company pursued *that* course, the Sizzler restaurant chain would have long since ceased to exist.

However, digging one's self out of a hole, no matter how successful such a task is accomplished, is no way to run a company. The right thing to do, of course, is to be proactive and obviate the growing weaknesses and threats that, if left unattended, will wreak havoc on the organization. The process by which this is accomplished is *Strategic Planning*. By this I mean a commitment to the genuine article—not four days at a mountain retreat whence management returns with 'the plan.' That's not strategic planning. That's nothing more than self-delusion. Recall my discussion in Chapter 5 of Hugh Duncan's Strategic Plan which apparently, he developed in solitude over a three or four-week period. Such a process inevitably leaves the planners feeling good about themselves and what they accomplished but also, just as inevitably, the beneficial results of their efforts, if any, usually dissipate fairly quickly. The strategic planning to which I refer entails an arduous process which can easily be extended out over many months, perhaps even a year or more, involve hundreds of hours of effort on the part of the senior management planning committee plus many others outside that group for a company Sizzler's pre-bankruptcy size.

Also, recall in Chapter 5, the efforts of the National Sizzler Franchisee Association to introduce the strategic planning process to Dick Birmingham and Jim Collins. The effort failed for a number of reasons but one in particular I believe is because the effort was viewed as an event—the planning meeting—that was supposed to produce a tangible result—the plan. What was missed, was the fact that the *process* by which the plan should be developed is really where the greatest value in strategic planning is derived. Our strategic planning facilitator, Reb Gooding, tried to make this fact clear during the course of the demonstration exercise but it didn't happen. Another thing that didn't happen was an appreciation for the importance of various elements of the strategic planning process. Everyone more or less got behind the development of a mission statement, but seemed to jump from that point to developing action plans to accomplish the mission. I've seen this phenomenon a lot in various planning processes I have encountered and what tends to be glossed over is the middle part of the process. Specifically, I mean the S.W.O.T. analysis.

The acronym S.W.O.T. stands for Strengths, Weaknesses, Opportunities and Threats. A "S.W.O.T." analysis is essentially a performance audit, the intent of which is to assess how well or poorly the company as a whole and senior management in particular are doing across a broad range of management imperatives. Accomplishing this project in a comprehensive way is no minor feat. It can be the most time consuming and difficult part of the process if done well. From my experience, I can say that this task is the one most subject to the extreme danger of being hastily compiled based on unsubstantiated management assumptions, anecdotal information and recent financial performance data. In a letter I sent to Dick Birmingham in nineteen ninety-two, I suggested the company engage in this effort. I pointed out what a central role the performance audit had come to be in Sizzler's culture at the operating unit level and suggested that by logical extension of this culture, perhaps the organization as a whole could benefit equally as well from such an exercise. I suggested the company measure its performance against the standards of management excellence established in the Malcolm Baldrige Award criteria. Recall in Chapter Five, my discussion on this point. My principal concern was with the quality and style of leadership currently being exhibited but I saw additional opportunities for the company to become more sensitized to many of its other weaknesses as well. Also recall that my suggestion was not well received.

In fairness to Dick Birmingham, I must confess that the NSFA's efforts to encourage our franchisor to engage in strategic planning and my suggestion that the company submit itself to a performance audit were more than a little late in coming. I don't think the kind of strategic planning process I have suggested here including a comprehensive performance audit are the most appropriate or practical tools to employ in a time of crisis because there is just too much pressure on senior management to find a quick fix. Unfortunately, short of filing for bankruptcy as Sizzler did, I don't know what other course of action would have been available to a company in Sizzler's predicament by nineteen ninety-two that could have predictably enabled it to extricate itself from its dilemma. One can only wonder at this point how things could have evolved differently had the company developed a sound planning culture in the early to mid-nineteen-eighties at the latest and therewith, in theory at least, proactively identified and addressed the weaknesses in the company's command and control systems which eventually became overwhelming.

This brings me to the second debilitating weakness that I believed conspired to bring about Sizzler's collapse. That weakness was an *Incorrect Strategic Focus*.

I believe Sizzler management was far too narrowly focused on the center of the plate as the means by which to perpetually reinvigorate its ongoing ability to establish and maintain a competitive advantage. Sizzler seemed to me to have what could best be described as a product driven mind set--meaning that so long as the products offered continued to be innovative, they would remain viable. In looking back over Sizzler's forty-year history, however, there are only two occasions where a new product introduction *per se* significantly spurred sales and that was the introduction of the Sizzler Salad Bar and Steak and All-You-Can-Eat-Shrimp. Of course, many of the other products Sizzler introduced no doubt had some positive influence on sales--especially in the nineteen-seventies when the chain added Steak & Lobster and Prime Rib. However, I believe the forces that moved Sizzler forward were not primarily the introduction of new products.

The first innovation--the one that launched the Sizzler chain in the first place--was Del and Helen Johnson's innovative merchandising and discount pricing of steak dinners. Top Sirloin and New York cut steak dinners were certainly not novel ideas. But figuring out how to sell them for a dollar and make a profit in the process was a tremendous innovation. In fact, their idea didn't just spawn a restaurant chain, it spawned an entire industry--the Budget Steak House industry.

The second innovation and first real change--and I believe the *only* real change--made to the operational system first developed by the Johnsons was Sizzler International's modification of the kitchen-to-customer product delivery system. Under the original format, each customer was given an order pick-up number. When a customer's meal was ready, one of the cooks would announce the pick-up number over the public address system and the customer had to go up to the pick-up window retrieve his meal and return to his table. This was changed in the mid nineteen-seventies with the introduction of Sizzler Dining Room Service. Essentially, a wait staff was added that performed the identical product delivery task for the customer. Various embellishments were added to the Sizzler Wait Staff's customer service requirements over the years but in-and-of themselves cannot be regarded as substantial changes.

The third thing that propelled Sizzler forward was its ability to break through the Television Advertising threshold in its major markets--initially in the greater Los Angeles region and the San Francisco Bay Area. This ability was the single most compelling reason for me to be a Sizzler franchisee. In the advertising business there is a term often referred to called TOMA meaning Top of Mind Awareness. The idea behind this term is that generally speaking, consumers only keep the name of three bands, at most, of any product they buy in their conscious memory at any given time and, moreover, a greater market share will almost always accrue to the brands with the most widespread Top of Mind Awareness among the consuming public. Thus, there is fierce competition among retailers to acquire Top of Mind Awareness for their brand and there is an enormous amount of research that goes on in the market place to find out which brand names for various products have a Top-of-Mind Awareness position with a significant portion of the population. For years, Sizzler enjoyed a Top-of-Mind awareness position among the vast majority of the population in its major markets and we knew it.

The fourth thing that helped build Sizzler was its first and only truly successful repositioning effort when the company and all its franchisees remodeled their units in the late nineteen-seventies and early nineteen-eighties.

The fifth and sixth forces which elevated the chain came into place more or less simultaneously with the system's image upgrading process. Those were the introduction of the Sizzler Salad Bar pioneered by Jack Williams and the implementation of the Store Performance Audit program developed by Walt Fitzgerald.

The last innovation to have any noticeable positive affect on Sizzler's per store average sales was the introduction of Steak and All-You-Can-Eat Shrimp but this idea had about a five-year life. Steak and All-You-Can-Eat Shrimp was introduced in the early nineteen-eighties. After that, nothing Sizzler tried had any long term significant positive impact on Per Store Average Sales. All subsequent increases in system-wide sales were due either to price increases or the addition of more operating units or increases in advertising.

Perhaps one of the best books written about the food service industry which was addressed primarily to the CEOs of the nation's multi-unit restaurant chains was *Fast Food: The Endless Shakeout* by Robert L. Emerson. At the time his book was published, Mr. Emerson was the Vice President of Fred Alger & Company and as a securities analyst, his specialty was the fast-food industry, a segment of the food service industry in which Sizzler was, by his definition, a part. In it he wrote

> ...attempts to build sales or traffic per store by way of adding new products to broaden the range of consumer appeal, can often disturb the delicate image of the chain in the consumer's mind and actually cause declines in sales and profitability. Moreover, operating problems caused by expansion of menus can lower profit margins.[47]

The most forceful reiteration of this proposition came in the interview he included in his book with Kentucky Fried Chicken's Chairman, Richard Mayer, the individual whom Mr. Emerson describes as "having transformed Kentucky Fried Chicken from a floundering operation to one that has in the past three years, roughly nineteen seven-seven to nineteen eighty shown among the most consistent patterns of sales growth in the industry." To quote Richard Mayer

---

[47] Robert L. Emmerson, *Fast Food: The Endless Shakeout,*

...when you proliferate a menu...you typically don't add incremental volume; what you do is just split it. It's rare that you find incremental volume.in a day part. It's one of the cancers of the industry: not understanding incremental versus cannibalistic volume...Specialize, get high product turnover, maintain quality, efficiency and good profitability...Those kinds of principles, I think, the Colonel brought to chicken. He used to go crazy when he went into a franchisee's store who had too many items on the menu. "Make chicken properly," he used to say, "and you'll do very well, thank you!" What the Colonel was saying was simply specialize with the highest quality products and you'll have high customer [counts] and product turnover. High turnover leads to quality. If you lower the turnover of your products by having a broad menu, as we had been doing, the quality goes down, the customer counts go down, profits go away. It's an insidious slide.[48]

I read this book in early nineteen eighty-four, shortly after Sizzler rolled out Operation Crow's Nest. There were two principal features to this operation. One was to add fresh fish to Sizzler's menu and the other was to eliminate most product photographs and reduce the type face size on Sizzler's wall hung menu board thereby increasing potential number of menu items that could be featured. This was a concern to me and in two letters I sent to Mike Minchin in the Spring of nineteen eighty-four I pointed this out as emphatically as I could. I even included a photo copy of the page in Emersion's book with the foregoing statement by Richard Mayer. In my second letter to Mike Minchin in May nineteen eighty-four I said the new menu board is going to open the flood gates on product proliferation. If any one thing about Operation Crow's Nest needs to be more thoroughly considered, that new menu board is it. I think within it lies the potential to cause irreversible harm to Sizzler's reputation.

I made this statement several years before a number of management experts published books which pretty much said the same thing. To wit:

> The temptation to blur a generic strategy, and therefore become stuck in the middle, is particularly great for a focuser once it has dominated its target segments. Focus involves deliberately limiting potential sales volume. Success can lead a focuser to lose sight of the reasons for its success and compromise its focus strategy for growth's sake.[49]
> Michael Porter

To avoid getting stuck in the middle you must out niche your competitors, you've got to 'focus, focus, focus'... There is a difference between niche

---

[48] *Ibid.,* p.

[49] Michael Porter, *Competitive Advantage* (copyright 1985, The Free Press, New York, N.Y.) p. 17.

marketing and product churning. Product churning is coming out with new products and services to expand sales. Period. It's not coming out with clearly differentiated products or services for clearly defined niches.[50]
Robert E. Linneman, Ph.D. and John L. Stanton, Jr., Ph.D.

...Today, as in Henry Ford's era, variety kills efficiency. Ford maintained a very narrow product line. He didn't introduce a variant of the Model T until millions of units of the basic model had been produced. As for variety in color, he left posterity his legendary remark: "Any color you want as long as its black." Operationally excellent companies reject variety, because it burdens the business with cost. They produce no-frills products for the middle of the market where demand is huge and customers are more interested in cost than in choice...Undisciplined companies, on the other hand, let products and services proliferate. They create a variant in response to one customer or operational demand, then create another to fill a different niche.[51]
Michael Treacy & Fred Wiersema

The central point of the foregoing was to get to the essence of what I believe to be Senior Sizzler Management's second fundamental weakness.

That being that Sizzler's underlying principal strategic focus was the continuing implementation of *Offensive Competitive Tactics* when the company should have primarily focused on the use of *Defensive Competitive Tactics.*

By Offensive Competitive Tactics I mean efforts to try to add incremental customers to the existing customer base by way of adding new products that would pull them away from the competition and into a Sizzler. On the other hand, by Defensive Competitive Tactics I mean efforts to hold on to Sizzlers' core customers and otherwise protect its market niche from the offensive efforts of *its* competitors.

This is not to say that Sizzler *never* employed defensive tactics or *always* employed offensive tactics. My premise is that the company devoted significantly more resources toward offensive activities than defensive activities when it should have been the other way around. Nor is it to say that successful offensive tactics worked less well than successful defensive tactics. Indeed, under my interpretation of these terms, both the

---

[50] Robert E. Linneman, Ph.D. and John L. Stanton, Jr., Ph.D. *Making Niche Marketing Work* (copyright 1991, McGraw-Hill, Inc.) pages 7 and 85.

[51] Michael Treacy & Fred Wiersema *The Discipline Of Market Leaders* (Copyright 1995, Addison-Wesley Publishing Company) p. 49.

introduction of the Sizzler Salad Bar and Steak and All-You-Can-Eat Shrimp are examples of successful offensive tactics.

However, the success of those two product introductions notwithstanding, the fact remains that they were the *only* new product introductions in the company's history that successfully produced a measurable increase in customers. In my opinion, the introduction of Sizzler Dining Room Service, the remodeling of the stores and the Store Performance Audit program are all examples of successful defensive tactics.

Having said that, I am well aware that my entire premise regarding Sizzler's strategic focus and the examples I have provided to support my argument are wide open to different interpretations. I have no doubt that opponents to my view can make compelling arguments that any of the above examples are the opposite of how I portrayed them. Yet, that's how I see it.

Examples of Sizzler's failure to commit sufficient resources or thought to defensive tactics abound. There are a few that stand out in my mind as most pronounced. First is the fact that the Sizzler chain taken as a whole never developed the capability to produce an order of French fries that the customer could depend upon to be cooked properly and be cooked the same no matter what Sizzler he or she visited and no matter how many times he or she visited the same Sizzler. This was a pet peeve of mine for years and all I could do was try to reach this mile stone within the stores I owned. I don't believe I ever reached it but I think I came closer than most. I look at McDonalds with envy on this point. That company, in my opinion, has refined the capability to accomplish this seemingly simple but actually quite difficult task better than any restaurant or restaurant chain in the country.

Another example is the equally undependable quality of the baked potatoes Sizzler served--not to mention the lack of dependability in having them available at all. Again, I believe that was a serious problem and a solvable one, if the company would have devoted sufficient resources to it.

One would think that being a steak house chain Sizzler's size would have devoted significant resources to the development of an ideal cooking surface for the type and size of steaks we served and additionally considered the skill level of the typical Sizzler cook and marketing aspects relating to cooking methods. If you think that, you would be wrong. Throughout Sizzler's history up to the time I left the organization there was an ongoing debate as to whether our steaks should be cooked over an open flame or on a slightly inclined solid hot metal surface. The fact is that roughly half the Sizzlers in the country cooked them one way and half the other. In addition, there were always problems with cooking surface temperature recovery as steaks were constantly put on and taken off the cooking surface which were never satisfactorily resolved with the equipment we had available.[52]

On a more ethereal level I believe that Sizzler never really understood the meaning of concept positioning or what causes this process to occur despite the fact that from nineteen ninety on, that was frequently a central topic of discussion and press releases. In Christopher Thomas's interview with Greig Patterson cited previously, Mr. Thomas made the statement that "Sizzler has repositioned itself three or four times over the company's 35-year history." Sizzler may have tried to reposition itself this many times and may even have believed that it succeeded in that effort but I don't think that ever happened. Concept Positioning while being a corporate strategic action, does not necessarily become an accomplished fact once the various steps involved in the process have been completed. A restaurant's concept position or any branded product's image in the market place relative to its competitors is a phenomenon that *exists only in the mind of the consumer*. "Positioning is not what you do to a product. Positioning is what you do to the mind of the customer."[53] No matter how a restaurant chain wants to be regarded by the consuming public and no matter what it does to create a specific image of itself in the consuming public's mind, this means nothing if the consuming public doesn't see it that way.

I think Sizzler has held three distinct image positions in the mind of the consumer and only repositioned itself twice. The first position was the one created from its inception as a budget steak house. The second was a modification to that image subsequent to its massive remodeling efforts in the early nineteen-eighties. With this change, I believe Sizzler became regarded as a Classy Budget Steak and Salad Bar restaurant. That repositioning effort was by design and, in my opinion, was the only time that an intended repositioning effort achieved the desired results.

Sizzler's third repositioning was accidental and I think the process began prior to the introduction of the Buffet Court. I believe that throughout the nineteen-eighties Sizzler had managed to gradually and imperceptibly erode its credibility as a Budget steak house as it proceeded to use an ever-increasing cost-to-retail markup multiplier. The image confusion caused by that process was further compounded, I believe, by the chain's propensity to focus on relatively small portion sizes for its steaks. This was done to keep the retail price as low as possible while at the same time using the higher multiplier. The consequence of this action, I think, caused an erosion in people's perception of Sizzler as a place to go to get a good steak dinner. Moreover, I believe this blurring of Sizzler's image was compounded by two other factors.

---

[52] Along with the introduction of Sizzler's premium steak menu additions in October, 1997 the company announced plans to retrofit their restaurants with the new "clam shell" grill which is the state-of-the-art in commercial steak cookery. See *Nation's Restaurant News,* November 24, 1997.

[53] Al Ries and Jack Trout, *Positioning: The Battle For Your Mind*, Warner Books, Copyright 1986, p. 2.

The first of these additional two factors was Sizzler's totally unpublicized program it called Profit Enhancement. This program was introduced to the system at Sizzler's convention in San Diego in nineteen eighty-eight. The central element of the program was to enhance profits by lowering quality. That's not quite the spin the company put on the program, but that was the essence of the idea. Central to Profit Enhancement, were such things as the substitution of freshly cut lettuce with pre-cut lettuce, meaning lettuce cut by the vendor and shipped in plastic bags. This product did not have the visual appearance of freshness nor the crispness of lettuce iced down and cut daily in the store. Also included in the program were the substitution of other pre-cut vegetables for vegetables previously cut fresh daily in-store. To this was added the substitution of melted margarine for melted butter to be served with Sizzler's crab, lobster and other shell fish products and the substitution of imitation sour cream for the real thing to be served on the baked potatoes. All corporate stores transformed themselves in this way, however many franchisees, including myself, chose not to buy into this program.

The other factor I believe contributed to the erosion of Sizzler's image was the high repetition of Steak and All-You-Can-Eat Shrimp advertising from the mid nineteen-eighties through the early nineteen-nineties. I think the over dependence on this product as its primary promotional vehicle beginning around nineteen eighty-nine caused more harm to Sizzler's credibility for serving quality products than anyone has ever imagined. Tom Gregory was well aware of this gradual blurring of Sizzler's image. In an interview with a correspondent from *Nation's Restaurant News* in nineteen ninety-one he said "Sizzler is not a steak house, not a seafood restaurant, but something the public likes a lot."[54] He should have added, "but not as much as they used to." I believe the introduction of the Buffet Court put the capstone on Sizzler's unintended gradual repositioning process and finally crystallized Sizzler's image in consumers' minds. Perhaps this third and last repositioning of the restaurant chain's image was best described by Michael Mueller of San Francisco's Montgomery Securities who said "many of Sizzler's new diners were there because they just wanted to eat a lot. The gluttons helped change Sizzler in the public's eye from a casual, mid-price grill to a place for pigging out cheap."[55]

The point of the foregoing, taken as a whole, I believe helps make my case that Sizzler's predominant focus was not on protecting its turf; not on building and protecting a competitive advantage through a precisely defined and successfully executed positioning strategy. Sizzler's principal strategic focus was not on the implementation of defensive tactics as I think it should have been.

---

[54] *Nation's Restaurant News,* June 24, 1991, Volume 25, No. 25, p. 7

[55] *Financial World,* July 7, 1992 Volume 161, No. 14, p.14

It's ironic in a way that I hold this view while at the same time blaming the company's Board of Directors for allowing it to occur. I say this because the only company Director I ever met, besides Jim Collins, was UCLA's world-renowned coach John Wooden, who made a formal presentation to Sizzler's management and franchisees at our Lake Tahoe convention in nineteen seventy-four. In his presentation, which has probably long since been forgotten by most people in the Sizzler organization, is that the key to a successful competitive strategy lies principally in defense.

The last issue I want to address is how to interpret Sizzler's move into the Buffet Court in terms of offensive or defensive strategy. Was it offensive or was it defensive? Or, was it both? Or, was it neither?

In my interview with Mike Minchin. I quoted him as saying "the Buffet Court is a unique opportunity to rebuild the value perception of Sizzler, both among current and prospective customers." From this, I gather that this change in the Sizzler format was perceived as both an offensive and defensive move. In hind sight though, the Buffet Court appears to have brought in some new customers but drove off far more old customers. Without regard to the *a priori* perceived strategic effect of the Buffet Court, *a posteriori* I think one must conclude it was a purely offensive tactic--the ultimate of cost of which far exceeded the benefits.

Hindsight makes this interpretation fairly easy to argue. However, in the heat of the battle with no crystal ball to see into the future, making these kinds of interpretations by simply by applying experience, judgment and logic is flat out impossible. I think the lesson to be learned here is (1) verbalize your intended strategic tactic and (2) test it properly before implementation.

For all the criticism I have leveled at the way Tom Gregory and Mike Minchin managed the Sizzler Restaurant Chain, the fact remains that over the roughly twelve years they worked together they presided over a quadrupling of the system's total sales revenue, a tremendous appreciation in the company's stock value and the advancement of the company's positive reputation among the consuming public and stock analysts. On balance it's hard to argue that they were not capable senior managers. Moreover, with the trials and tribulations, details, distractions, and inevitable crises that demand practical and immediate solutions which are the constant companion of those charged with the day-to-day management of any organization, it's not easy to elevate oneself above it all to contemplate let alone act on such esoteric issues as company mission, management philosophy, corporate culture, company values, strategic focus and the like. They don't have the time to go to school either through home study or otherwise to constantly keep abreast of the latest thinking in the practice of management. Neither do they have the patients, typically, to translate the cumulative significance of their daily decisions into their strategic implications nor contemplate the long term affects thereof.

For a company the size of Sizzler, I think those are the sort of the issues the Board of Directors should assume the responsibility to consider and the sort of contribution the Board should make or initiate. Yet in Sizzler's case, based on my observations of the Board's failure to deal effectively, or indeed, to deal at all with the issues of senior management succession planning or the misadventures of Dick Birmingham, I do not believe they would have nonetheless devoted attention to those lofty concepts. In my view, becoming a member of Sizzler's Board of Directors was more akin to joining an exclusive country club than in assuming the almost sacrosanct fiduciary responsibility to be the ultimate guardian of stock holders' and franchisees' investments in the company plus the careers and retirement funds of its employees.[56] What kind of thought process or discussion preceded the approval of Hugh Duncan as Sizzler's President, the approval of Dailey & Associates as the company's new advertising agency, approving Dick's request that his wife Martha become a Sizzler Franchisee and the eventual buy back of her Sizzler, the continued endorsement of Dick Birmingham as Sizzler's Chief Executive or the approval of Kevin Perkins as Dick Birmingham's successor is something no one outside the Boardroom will ever know of course, but to my dying day, I will ask myself what on earth were they thinking.

At the very top of the organizational pyramid resides the Chairman of the Board of Directors, and everything I said about the fiduciary responsibility of the Board as a whole goes double for the Board Chairman. It's an awesome responsibility as is the responsibility to properly select those who will join him at the round table. Some say Jim Collins reluctance to dismiss Dick Birmingham was due to his intense loyalty to Dick. I believe otherwise. I don't see anything noble in Jim Collins' failure to replace Dick at all. In my opinion, loyalty to Dick was not the compelling reason Jim didn't replace him; in my opinion the motivation was a self-serving desire to avoid the pain and discomfort attendant in letting a long term, dedicated employee go. That is *very* hard to do; I know because I have done it. To the best of my knowledge and from accounts I have heard over the years from other senior managers in the Sizzler organization, Jim Collins had never fired a person in his life. But if this example of Jim's self-serving inclination is not sufficiently compelling, consider this: Jim Collins is an enormously wealthy man and his fortune is not at risk should Sizzler disappear altogether. In his capacity as Chairman of the Board of Sizzler he received a Director's Fee of $60,000 a year. In addition, Jim was drawing funds from Sizzler's retirement program as a retired executive. His principal source of income, almost up to the time the company declared bankruptcy, was from Sizzler stock dividends. However, realizing that the dividend paying days for Sizzler were numbered, just prior to declaring bankruptcy Jim came out of retirement and went back on the payroll, taking an annual salary of $200,000 a year. I realize that $200,000 a year one way or the other will not significantly affect Sizzler's ability to survive or not, however the symbolism in that action bespeaks, I believe, for Jim Collins' lack of a sense

[56] Sizzler's Retirement Plan for its employees is an "unfunded" plan meaning the source of cash to make monthly payments to its retirees will be from future earnings.

114

of responsibility or remorse for what has occurred. A lot of good people were financially ruined by Sizzler's collapse and I believe the Board of Directors is most to blame. The lesson in Sizzler's story for Corporate Directors is, stay alert. What happened to Sizzler is not so unique it can't happen again. These Directors were the most responsible for the collapse of an empire and if I can have my wish, this will be their legacy.

Endnote
September, 2021
The story told here encompasses the Sizzler restaurant chain's history from nineteen fifty-eight through nineteen ninety-six. As such, nothing said in this book should in any way be perceived as commentary regarding the current nature or circumstances of this company.